PROVEN
WHITETAIL TACTICS

GREG MILLER

Published by

700 E. State Street • Iola, WI 54990-0001
Telephone: 715/445-2214

Please call or write for our free catalog of outdoor publications. Our toll-free
number to place an order or obtain a free catalog is 800-258-0929 or please use
our regular business telephone 715-445-2214 for editorial comment
and further information.

ISBN: 0-87341-509-4
Printed in the United States of America

Photography by Greg Miller and Jeff Miller
Pen-and-ink drawings by Chuck Miller

Dedication

To my daughter and future hunting partner, Jessie Lyn.

Contents

Acknowledgments

First and foremost, I thank God. His continual blessings have made all this possible.

A special 'thank you' to my wife, Geralyn. You never cease to amaze me. Without a doubt, you're the most understanding, unselfish and compassionate person I know. My love for you continues to grow with each passing day.

Thank you to my children, Jacob and Jessie Lyn. You help me remain humble and appreciative of the truly special things in life.

To my brothers, Jeff, Mike and Jim—I thank you! I couldn't have been blessed with better hunting partners and friends.

Thanks so much to my dad. Your beautiful pen-and-ink drawings have added a very special touch to this book.

Thanks also to my mother. Your constant encouragement has kept me going through a lot of not-so-good times.

Lastly, a very special thank you to the many deer hunters out there who continue to read my articles, attend my seminars and, in other ways, encourage me to keep doing what I'm doing. I wish I could somehow personally thank each and every one of you!

About the Author

Greg Miller is a hard-core deer hunter from west-central Wisconsin. He has consistently taken large whitetail bucks with gun and bow for more than 30 years. Interestingly, many of Greg's bucks have been taken from public forests and farmlands. Because of this, he feels uniquely qualified to explain strategies that will work for other hunters.

Along with chasing big bucks in his home state, Greg has also hunted whitetails in the northern states of Montana, Minnesota, Michigan, Iowa, Illinois and Nebraska. Greg also has enjoyed a bit of success on southern whitetails. In the past, he has taken big bucks in Georgia, Alabama and Texas. In addition, he has hunted extensively in the western-Canadian provinces of Alberta and Manitoba.

Greg's biggest bow-killed buck to date is an 18-point non-typical that had a gross score of 202-5/8. The bruiser deer was shot during Wisconsin's 1990 late-archery season. A 13-point, 180-3/8 typical ranks as Greg's largest gun-killed buck.

Greg was employed as a seasonal construction worker for nearly 18 years. However, a serious injury in 1993 forced him to "retire" from that trade. He now makes his living as a full-time freelance outdoor writer/photographer, seminar speaker and book author.

Introduction

The response generated by my first book, **Aggressive Whitetail Hunting**, has made me aware of a very interesting fact. There are a whole lot of deer hunters out there who have progressed to the point where they no longer place any faith in "sure-fire gimmicks" or "can't-miss tactics." Like me, these individuals have learned that when hunting for big whitetail bucks, a common sense approach is their best ally.

I'm sure you'll realize quite quickly that this book definitely wasn't written in a fancy style. Rather, it was written in a straightforward manner. No filler. No fluff. Just good ol' common sense deer hunting stuff. (That's the way I write—a lot like the way I hunt, I might add!)

Of course, there's no guarantee that merely reading this book will put you within range of a monster buck each and every time you step into the woods. Regardless of what you might have heard, no such cure-alls exist. As with the my first book, the information in the following pages is meant to be used as reference material—nothing more.

One other thing. I'm sure anyone who has ever talked whitetails with me quickly was made aware of the great passion I harbor for these grand animals. And if you talked long enough with me, no doubt you also know that of all the methods one might employ to harvest trophy deer, I definitely prefer bowhunting over all else. This us exactly why the majority of this book deals with bowhunting strategies.

But I think it's terribly important to mention that I still spend a certain amount of time each year chasing whitetails with a firearm. I also take advantage of some of the special muzzle-loader deer seasons offered by several states. Although some self-proclaimed bowhunting purists might find this a bit disturbing, I still truly love to gun-hunt for big bucks.

The reason for my mentioning this is quite simple. You see, I'm of the opinion that far too many modern-day trophy whitetail hunters have developed "pigeon-hole" mentalities. By this I mean they either *only* bow hunt or they *only* gun hunt. To be honest, some of these individuals are very adamant (and a bit arrogant I might add) about stressing the fact that they are *specialized* trophy whitetail hunters.

I make no such claim. In fact, I prefer to say that I'm a deer hunter, plain and simple. I'd like to add that the strategies outlined in the following pages are designed to help other such deer hunters—those who are dedicated, persistent and willing to use a bit of common sense—to become a bit more successful. As far as I'm concerned, that's the most any of us can expect.

CHAPTER ONE

Dedication and Persistence

I'm fortunate in that I've been able to harvest a good number of mature whitetail bucks over the past 30-plus years. But I think it's important to mention that no single tactic is responsible for the demise of all those deer. In truth, I've employed a number of different tactics to bag my many trophies. None of these tactics would have been effective, however, if I hadn't first taken it upon myself to become fairly knowledgeable about every aspect of white-tailed deer behavior.

Yes, I feel strongly that acquiring a good deal of knowledge about your intended quarry is important. And I'm of the belief that you should be fairly well-versed in a number of different hunting strategies. But I don't consider any amount of knowledge about my hunting techniques or the animals I'm pursuing to be the most important reasons for my past success. Rather, my best allies have been absolute dedication and a very persistent attitude. A lot of my hunts have ended with the score in my favor simply because I've outlasted a certain buck.

Recently, I gave a seminar to a large group of deer hunters. After finishing the seminar, I was confronted with a question I've never before been asked. A member of the audience wanted to know if there was one single factor that has been *most* responsible for my success on taking mature whitetails.

Initially, the question caught me slightly off guard. But after thinking about it for just a few seconds, I knew exactly what my answer should be. "My attitude," I told him. "Without a doubt, my success with big whitetails is directly attributable to a never-say-die attitude. I remain very dedicated and persistent throughout the entire season."

Later, I started thinking about the way I had answered the guy's question. But even after I had turned it over countless times in my mind, I still came to the same conclusion. Certainly, a thorough understanding of white-tailed deer and deer behavior has helped immensely. And being fairly proficient at a number of different hunting techniques is a strong asset. However, there's no doubt that when it comes to hunting trophy whitetails, dedication and persistence are my strongest attributes. I had, indeed, given the perfect answer.

Much has been written and spoken about the many ways to become consistently successful hunting mature bucks. To be honest, most of this information can prove to be beneficial for those aspiring to up their track record on big bucks. And certainly, coupling this type of information with practical in the field experiences can put you well on your way to a higher success rate. But in the end, it's my opinion that dedication and persistence are the best weapons in *any* deer hunter's arsenal.

In the past few years, I've had the opportunity to hunt and/or talk with some of the most successful deer hunters in North America. Almost to a man, these hunters would readily admit that the key to their success is a strong "get out there and get after 'em" attitude. Oh sure, most of them have honed their deer-hunting skills to a fine edge. And they're proficient at several different methods for taking whitetails. But when it comes right down to the nitty-gritty, these guys trust persistence and dedication to consistently put them in position to harvest mature bucks.

Over the past 12 years I've written several hundred magazine articles about hunting for white-tailed deer. In addition, during the past six years I've given seminars at some of the largest deer shows in the country. This exposure has given me the chance to talk to literally hundreds of deer hunters. One thing has become apparent from these many talks. There are a lot of deer hunters who think there are shortcuts to becoming consistently successful at taking mature whitetails. But take it from someone who has been playing this game a *long* time. There are no shortcuts!

I'm sure most people have heard the old saying, "patience is a virtue." Well, when it comes to hunting for trophy whitetails, I'm a firm believer that dedication and persistence are a blessing. As mentioned, it's my never-say-die approach to the sport that has put me in position to take many of my biggest bucks to date. Once I was able to figure out where a big buck was living, I'd then go about learning his habits and special little quirks. In many instances, it was only a matter of time before a buck I'd targeted would walk by within range.

I should explain something here. When I say it was only a matter of time, this doesn't necessarily mean I was successful at taking a big buck during the first season I hunted him. To be honest, there have been several instances where I've chased a particular buck for a couple of years before I got even my first glimpse of him. And then maybe he wasn't within range or in sight long enough to get off a shot. However, there also have been a few that wandered just a little too close and stayed within sight just a little too long.

A dedicated and persistent approach is a key ingredient for consistent success on mature bucks.

Hunting Where the Bucks Are

Your dedicated and persistent attitude must be applied in areas that harbor good populations of antlered animals. And if you're a strict trophy hunter, then it's definitely to your advantage if the areas you're hunting have established a reputation of producing mature bucks. Let's face it, trying to harvest a trophy buck from an area where there are no trophy bucks is going to be extremely difficult—no matter how much time you put into the sport!

Believe it or not, I still see a lot of deer hunters making this very basic mistake. No doubt they possess the abilities to take monster whitetails. They also display great dedication and persistence. Unfortunately, these guys are spending the greater part of their free time hunting in areas that just aren't conducive to high success rates—especially on mature whitetail bucks.

Knowing the habits and travel routes of individual bucks can be extremely beneficial, but I've often found that exposure is still my best ally. Many of my best bucks were taken simply because I out-waited those deer. The old adage of "you

Dedication and persistence are wasted commodities if you spend all of your time hunting in areas where there are no bucks.

can't shoot 'em if you aren't out there" certainly rings true here. However, it's also true that you can't shoot 'em if *they* aren't out there.

Recently, my brother Mike and I were discussing the finer points of hunting for trophy whitetails. During our conversation, Mike made a very interesting comment. "Yeah, persistence is definitely a strong attribute," my brother stated. "But all the persistence in the world isn't worth a hoot if you spend your time hunting in an area where there just aren't any big bucks." Truer words were never spoken.

During the past five years or so, I've had the opportunity to hunt with more than a few successful trophy whitetail hunters. If there's one single thing these guys all have in common it's that they have an enthusiasm for the sport I see in very few hunters. In a nutshell, they display an undying form of persistence. And just like the postman, these highly successful hunters don't let rain, sleet, snow or any other adverse conditions keep them from their appointed rounds. Like me, these guys refuse to admit defeat until the final bell sounds and the season comes to a close.

A hunt near Pine Mountain, Georgia, a few years back is a perfect illustration of what I'm talking about. Rain came down in buckets throughout the three days we were scheduled to hunt. Despite the horrid conditions, none of us on that hunt gave any thought to sitting in our comfortable cabins and waiting out the weather. We were up and out the door well before daylight each morning, braving the rain and cool temperatures. In the evening, it was off to a nearby Laundromat to dry our drenched clothing. Our persistence paid off, however, as each of us had connected on a decent buck by hunt's end.

Success Through Good Time Management

Dedication and persistence aren't qualities reserved only for those who have an enormous amount of time to dedicate to the sport. In fact, nothing could be further from the truth. It's entirely possible for anyone to adopt a dedicated and persistent attitude toward their hunting efforts, no matter if you're granted two days or five days a week to hunt.

In fact, it's my opinion that those with a limited amount of free time should be the first to develop a dedicated and persistent attitude. Since your free time is so precious, it only stands to reason that you should spend this time wisely. Allow me to give an example of exactly what I mean.

Some years back I decided that I wanted to devote a lot more time to deer hunting. Right off, I knew certain concessions would have to be made. Since my family's welfare was of utmost concern, I wouldn't be able to cut back on the number of hours I was putting in at my construction job. So I had to look elsewhere for some "extra" deer hunting time. As I discovered, it wasn't all that hard to find.

Along with chasing whitetails during the fall, I'd always had a love for hunting ruffed grouse, pheasants and waterfowl. But the decision to become a more serious trophy deer hunter meant giving up these pursuits. Like it or not, I knew the time had come to clean my shotgun and retire it to the gun cabinet. Worse, it meant my bird dog would suddenly become nothing more than a house pet. But I considered the trade-off more than fair. I simply had to rank my interests according to a very real set of priorities. The result was that I had more time to spend chasing large-racked whitetails.

The point I'm trying to get across is that anybody can employ a dedicated and persistent approach—even those of us who are granted only a small amount of free time. However, because of the very limited amount of free time we get, it's imperative we learn how to use every second of that time to our benefit.

Establish Multiple Stand Sites

One very important factor to keep in mind is that if you are fortunate enough to be able to spend an enormous amount of time hunting, not all that time should be spent at just one or two stand sites. The number of stand options you have should rise proportionately with the amount of time you spend hunting.

I like to have more than just a few stand options from which to choose—no matter how much time I get for hunting. I think this is where a lot of deer hunters run into trouble. They seem content with spending the entire season hunting from just a couple different stands. (In fact, I still know of many individuals who spend all their hunting time perched in one spot!) No matter how much time you spend hunting, it's important you have a number of different stand options at your disposal.

Now, this isn't to say you have to run all over the country looking for a bunch of different areas to hunt. Increasing your number of available stand sites might merely entail doing a little more looking around in the spots you're already hunt-

Establishing a good number of stand-sites is only the beginning. You must also acquire the discipline required to constantly rotate your hunting efforts.

ing. Usually, if the amount of available acreage is adequate, you should be able to locate several good stand sites on the same tract of land.

For instance, I dedicate a lot of my free time hunting one farm in particular. This farm is only 300 acres in size, yet I have more than two-dozen stand options at my disposal. As you might imagine, wind direction plays a large role in my decision as to what stand I occupy on a given day. But my decision is also swayed heavily by how much attention I've given a particular stand in recent days. The last thing I want to do is "burn-out" a potentially good area simply because I've over-hunted a certain stand.

Once you establish several different stands, it's important you then acquire the discipline needed to rotate your efforts. Its been my experience that most deer hunters have one stand they prefer to hunt more than any other. I don't know whether this frame of mind has been brought about by favorable past experiences or simply by the location of that stand. (Maybe visibility is great, or it's easy to get to, or comfortable, etc.) Regardless, adopting a persistent hunting attitude means you'll have to get out of the 'favorite stand' syndrome.

When it comes to rotating our hunting efforts, my hunting partners and I have adopted a strict regimen that we try to follow to the letter. We don't occupy any of our stands more than once every two or three days. Believe me, we've found that a strict adherence to this policy is in our best interest. Even if a deer happens to detect our presence, that deer will tend to forget about the ordeal if it doesn't encounter the same situation within the next day or two.

In those situations where we have a close encounter of the personal kind with a big buck, we avoid that area altogether for a minimum of five days. This five-day rest period gives both that particular buck and all the other deer in that area plenty of time to calm down and forget about the incident. Again, such an approach is especially crucial when in pursuit of older age-class whitetails.

I remember a certain mature whitetail buck I chased around in the big woods of northern Wisconsin. It took two years of dogged dedication and persistence before I was finally able to harvest the trophy animal. But even with the amount of pressure I put on the buck, I remain convinced to this day that he never really knew he was being hunted. That's because I had a half-dozen different stand sites scattered throughout the buck's core area. Yes, I put a lot of hours into hunting that particular deer. But because I constantly rotated my stand sittings, this "pressure" never came from one particular spot.

Another important fact: I never let my pursuit of that buck become an all-consuming thing. In other words, I didn't spend every bit of my available hunting time chasing that one buck. There were times when I'd leave the buck alone for many days. During those times I'd go off and hunt other deer in completely different areas. The final results speak well for this very evasive, yet persistent approach.

Dedication + Persistence = Success

My biggest bow-killed deer to date is another study in dedication and persistence. My brother Jeff and I hunted that monster deer for two years without ever

My brother and I hunted this monster buck for two full seasons, yet I'm convinced the deer never really knew we were after him. The trick is being dedicated and persistent without becoming careless.

once getting a "for sure" look at him. But even though the buck displayed a very reclusive and elusive nature, we didn't become frustrated.

Jeff and I continued to sit on stands in the heart of the big buck's core area. We only sat on those stands, however, when conditions were perfect. And we were constantly rotating our stand site locations. Finally, on a cold afternoon in December, the big non-typical made the mistake of walking by within bow range of one of my stands. Again, we were persistent without becoming careless. I'm convinced the big deer never really felt pressured.

One of the most important times to display a dedicated and persistent attitude, is when facing challenging weather. Extremely cold or hot temperatures cause some hunters to simply give up and wait for better conditions. But as stated earlier in this piece, the best in the sport don't let such things as weather cause even the slightest distraction. This is another subject I'll cover in greater detail in a later chapter.

It's important to note that merely increasing your time in the woods won't necessarily ensure an instantaneous rise in your success rate. However, I firmly believe that over the long haul successful seasons will start outnumbering unsuccessful ones. At that point, you'll surely cite your dedication and persistence as being directly responsible.

But perhaps this is the reason why dedication and persistence are such rare commodities these days. Far too many deer hunters just don't have the patience or mental discipline it takes to adopt this type of approach. Simply put, these individuals want success and they want it right now!

I believe even the most successful trophy whitetail hunters also go through periods of hesitation and doubt. It's human nature. I keep things in perspective by thinking about how great the final payoff can be. Believe me, there's no way of describing the sense of accomplishment you feel when you finally affix your tag to a monster buck.

Lastly, I should mention that a certain mental attitude is necessary before a dedicated and persistent approach should be considered. You've got to accept the fact that there will be far more unproductive than productive hunts. Remember, in most cases success makes up only a tiny sliver of the total amount of time we spend in pursuit of our intended quarry.

Call it what you want—persistence, dedication, endurance, perseverance or even bull-headedness (which is my wife's favorite term). But no matter what you call it, when it comes to achieving a consistent track record on mature whitetails, no single factor will be more beneficial than a dedicated and persistent attitude. And it's certainly a prerequisite for using the rest of the information found in the following chapters of this book.

Greg's Proven Pointers

- Acquiring a wealth of knowledge about your quarry is extremely important—but there's more to it than that.

- Hunters must couple their book-learned knowledge with an equal amount of "in-the-field" gathered knowledge.

- Adopting a persistent hunting approach means you'll have to get away from the "favorite stand syndrome."

- Far too many deer hunters don't have the patience or mental discipline it takes to adopt a dedicated and persistent approach. These people want success and they want it now!

- Take it from someone who has been playing this game a long time: there are no shortcuts! When it comes to pursuing mature bucks, dedication and persistence are a blessing.

CHAPTER TWO

Honing

Your Mental

Edge

I want to begin this chapter by making a statement I know is going to raise the hackles of more than just a few people. The majority of licensed deer hunters in North America will *never* reach a level where they will realize consistent success on mature whitetail bucks. In fact, I'd be willing to bet that it will be a struggle for many hunters to take even average-size bucks on a consistent basis. Most of these hunters will never know the pleasure of affixing their tag to just one bragging-size buck.

Although many trophy whitetail hunters make the claim of being dedicated and hard-core, it's my opinion that there are darn few who actually make the grade. I think I know why. When studied closer, the effort put forth by most self-proclaimed experts pales in comparison to the energy expended by those who truly are consistently successful at taking mature bucks. It goes further, however.

Becoming the envy of your local deer hunting community means paying some pretty hefty dues. As I stated in the first chapter, I take great pains to learn as much as possible about the animals I pursue. I also consider myself to be about as dedicated and persistent as they come. But as I've learned, dedication and persistence aren't worth a hoot if you have trouble keeping the proper mental outlook. This is where so many "wanna-be" trophy whitetail hunters are severely lacking.

Developing the Right Mental Outlook

In recent years especially, I've come to believe that the sort of mental outlook a person has can have a tremendous bearing on whether or not they will achieve success. And although I believe that keeping the proper frame of mind is important for all deer hunters, it's especially critical for those of us who chase white-tails with bow and arrow. Why do I feel this way? Well, it has a lot to do with the fact that bowhunters are using a weapon with a very limited effective range. Even the best archery shots in the world need to have their target fairly close before they'll be able to inflict a sure, killing shot.

What this means is that merely seeing a big buck is no guarantee that we'll get a shot. In fact, I've come to the conclusion that the bigger the buck, the less chance we have of getting a shot. Whether it's some sort of sixth sense or just plain luck, (or a combination of both) the most mature whitetails seem to have an uncanny ability to either stay just out of range or keep just enough obstruction between them and us to remain safe.

This probably wouldn't be so bad if experiences of this nature were rare. Unfortunately, they can be common occurrences—especially for those of us who are truly dedicated and persistent. Either you learn how to mentally deal with monster bucks continually giving you the slip or you don't progress as a hunter. It's that simple.

I've bowhunted with a bunch of guys who would get totally bent out of shape if they saw a big buck, but were unable to get a shot. You can just about imagine the sort of behavior these same individuals displayed if they were offered a shot and missed. As a sidenote, I can tell you that *none* of these guys have been the least bit successful at taking mature bucks. Of course, they blame their lack of success on many different things. But the truth of the matter is that they haven't developed the proper mental outlook it takes to become a highly successful whitetail hunter.

As an example of the sort of roller-coaster range of emotions bowhunters can expect to deal with, let me relate my experiences from a recent season. To begin with, I missed a huge buck while bow-hunting in Iowa the first of November. After reviewing the video tape of the incident (that's right, I had a camerman with me), there's no doubt in my mind the monster 14-pointer's rack would have gross-scored more than 180 typical points. How did I manage to miss such a magnificent creature? Simple. What I thought was a 20-yard shot turned out to be closer to 30 yards. My arrow skimmed just under the buck's chest. Oh well!

The following morning, with a cameraman once more in tow, I went right back out for another go-around with those big Iowa whitetails. About a half-hour after sunrise, I decided to try a bit of rattling. Several minutes after finishing my sequence, we heard a deer approaching through the frozen leaves. A dandy 10-point buck soon came walking into view. It seemed to take him forever to close the distance, but the big deer finally ended up within bow range. This time I didn't miss.

The following week found me chasing big bucks in Illinois. Although I had several borderline-size bucks walk by within spitting distance the first few days, I couldn't get a mature deer to make a fatal mistake. But that's not to say I didn't see some real hogs during this time. I saw at least a half-dozen trophy bucks, including one that dwarfed the big deer I'd seen in Iowa the week before. The world-class whitetail was tending a hot doe and passed by 75 yards from where I

Many deer hunters claim to be hard-working and dedicated, when, in reality, their efforts pale in comparison to consistently successful hunters.

sat perched in a huge old oak. By the way, I finally got a chance at a good buck on the final day of my hunt. Again, I underestimated the distance to my target.

A month later found me hunting near Sonora, Texas. This hunt would have been a snap—had I been carrying a rifle. But I had decided to try for one of those dainty little Texas whitetails with my bow. Over a three-day period I played hide-and-seek with several large bucks. On the final day of my hunt, I used my grunt call to coax a long-tined 8-pointer within 15-yards of my tripod stand. Standing at a perfect quartering away angle, the buck turned his head and looked away from me. I managed to draw my bow undetected and promptly sent a razor sharp broadhead through his lungs. At times this game can seem so easy!

Riding the Emotional Roller-Coaster

These stories pretty well sum up the point I'm trying to make: bowhunting for trophy whitetails can be a stressful endeavor. Over the course of a season we can experience hundreds of emotional highs and lows. As far as that goes, we can experience quite a range of emotions in just a few minutes. For example, let's say you're on your stand and a big buck walks into view 50 yards away. The buck stops and stands in the same spot for what seems like forever. The longer he stands there, the more convinced you become that he never will walk within bow range. Depressing!

Suddenly, the buck starts walking slowly toward your stand. He continues on until he's a mere twenty steps from your stand, at which point he turns broadside. The big deer continues walking along, and you manage to get to full draw unde-tected. Great! Then, just as you're lining up your sight pin, the buck stops walk-ing. This would be great, except for the fact that he stopped right behind a large tree. There's no way you can slip an arrow into his vitals. Depressing!

The buck remains behind the tree for nearly a minute, then starts walking again. Unfortunately, he changes his line of travel just a bit. Instead of continuing on in the direction he was originally heading, the buck is now walking straight away from you. Worse, he's keeping that big tree squarely between you and him. You can see his huge rack sticking out on both sides of the tree as he slowly walks out of range. Very depressing!

I'll agree, it can be very depressing to have a trophy buck within bow range and then not even get a shot at that buck. But as bowhunters we must quickly realize that this sort of thing is going to happen. Further, it probably is going to happen quite often. That's what I was talking about when I said that keeping the proper mental outlook is so critical for bow-hunters. (In many cases, gun-hunters are able to kill a buck the second he walks into view.) I've been playing this game a long time. If I've learned one thing it's that you can't let bad things that happened on past hunts ruin future hunts. Personally, I'm able to keep myself on a fairly even keel my remembering that there will always be another day. I've also found that it's wise to go easy on yourself. Unlike some hunters, I don't consider a missed chance or an actual missed shot at a big buck to be an unforgivable sin. You simply

Having a monster buck within bow range, and then having that deer walk off without offering a shot, can be a very depressing ordeal.

can't let bad experiences undermine your positive mental outlook. After all, we're only human.

Mentally Preparing for the Unexpected

I think that far too many deer hunters go into the woods with the idea that things are going to go exactly as they planned. Maybe you've extensively scouted a particular piece of property. And maybe you've also spent a number of hours just sitting back and watching the way the deer access that property when traveling about. By the time hunting season rolls around, you've figured out the travel routes of every buck on the property. You not only know exactly where those deer are going to walk, you also know exactly what time they'll be there. Or so you think...

So you sit on one of your strategically placed stands fully expecting a certain big buck to show up in a certain place at a certain time. And indeed a big buck does show up. But not only does he show up earlier than he's supposed to, he comes from a totally different direction. You quickly realize that the perfect shot scenario you've been dreaming of is not going to materalize.

In the 30 years I've been bow-hunting whitetails, I've seen very few shot opportunities in which everything was perfect. This has been especially true with most of the mature bucks I've had within bow range. I guess this can be attributed to the fact that big bucks seldom show up when they're supposed to, and they almost never walk where we want them to. So not only do they catch you off guard by appearing out of thin air, they further complicate matters by walking somewhere other than right into the ideal spot. Translated, this means your shot is going to be a bit more difficult than anticipated.

At times like this, you must be prepared to alter your game plan instantly. If you fail, it's most likely because you were unable to adjust to a suddenly different situation. Conversely, if you are successful, it's surely because you instantly recognized that things weren't going to go according to plan. Instead of pushing the panic button, you made the necessary adjustments and then an accurate shot.

I've hunted a lot of places with a number of different individuals during my many years of pursuing whitetails. Interestingly, I've become very good at immediately picking out the best hunters in camp and the "wannabes." Almost without fail, the "wannabes" own the most expensive and best of everything, including guns, bows, clothing, binoculars, footwear, etc. Sure, they're equipped to the teeth with the best equipment money can buy. And they can talk a good game.

But these guys are lacking perhaps the most crucial item necessary for serious hunters, and that is the proper mental outlook. This is made evident from their expression as they talk about big bucks that have managed to evade them. It's clear they take such things way too personal.

The best hunter in camp, on the other hand, usually has a bow or rifle that looks like it has seen its better days. Rather than looking abused, however, their weapon looks well-used. His clothing, although perfectly suited for the task, is well-worn and probably has a few rips and tears. One look at this guy's boots confirms that he isn't afraid to get out and do some leg work.

Overall, you can tell he's less concerned with how he looks and more concerned with what has worked for him in the past. It takes just a short conversation to confirm something more important. This guy has the proper mental outlook! Instead of gritting his teeth as he talks about big bucks that have eluded him, he smiles a sly little smile. That smile shows the respect he feels for a worthy opponent.

Interestingly, these guys display the same intensity and positive attitude on the last day of a week-long hunt that they showed on the very first morning. On the other hand, most "wannabe" hunters I've been in camp with display an increasing amount of pessimism as a hunt wears on. Heck, I've seen hunters of this description who are ready to throw in the towel after only a couple days. This is especially true if they think things aren't going their way.

So if on the final day of a week-long hunt each of the aforementioned hunters has a monster buck step out in front of them, which one do you think stands the best chance of killing that buck? Personally, I'm putting my money on the fellow with the beat up rifle, worn-out clothes and positive attitude!

Finding a Cure for Buck Fever

A chapter on the mental side of deer hunting wouldn't be complete without mentioning the most prevalent and commonly known mental affliction of deer hunters. I'm talking here about buck fever. In reality, none of what I've already covered in this chapter has any worth if you get so shaken at the sight of big buck that you have trouble thinking clearly.

If it's any consolation, I can tell you that I still get worked up when a monster buck is closing in on me. But I've come up with a little trick that helps me calm down in such situations. Basically, I keep telling myself over and over that something is going to happen to keep that big buck from coming within bow range. And if he does get within bow range, I then tell myself that something is going to happen to keep me from getting a shot.

Some may look at this as a negative mental outlook. All I can say to that is it works for me. I've found that if I can mentally convince myself I'm not going to get a shot, I'm usually fairly relaxed by the time I'm offered one.

Other hunters I've talked with have told me of little tricks they use to help them remain calm or even overcome buck fever. One guy told me that when he's got a big buck walking toward him, he pinches himself constantly on the side of the leg—and hard! Another bowhunter told me that he refuses to watch an approaching buck. Instead, he just sneaks quick glances at the deer until it is within bow range. Yet another fellow told me he forces himself to take at least 10 deep breaths.

Maybe you're one of the few bowhunters who have no problem staying calm and thinking straight when you've got a monster whitetail bearing down on your position. If you fit into this category, I honestly admire you. But if you're one of the many who have a problem keeping cool at the big moment, then you need to come up with your own little trick to help you stay mentally prepared.

No amount of expensive clothing and/or equipment will ensure success. Aspiring trophy hunters would be better advised to "invest" in the proper mental outlook.

I've learned another very important thing. In order to become a consistently successful trophy whitetail hunter, you must develop unwavering confidence in your abilities. But while confidence is terribly important, you must constantly guard against letting your confidence get out of control and turn into cockiness. While confidence is an attribute, cockiness usually is a detriment. Unfortunately, there's often such a fine line between the two that it can be difficult to tell when you've crossed over.

I look at it this way. You should be confident to the point that you fully expect to kill a big buck each and every time you go into the woods. However, if you're fortunate enough to kill a couple big bucks, that doesn't mean you can suddenly develop a different frame of mind.

I know several hunters who, after they managed to kill a good buck or two, allowed their confidence to spill over into cockiness. Yes, these guys were good hunters. But they were under the impression they were so good, that they really didn't have to try anymore. I'll give you one guess as to what happened to their success rates from that point forward.

Keeping the Home Fires Burning

There's one aspect of keeping the proper mental outlook I've never seen addressed, yet it could well be the most important for serious whitetail hunters. It has to do with your relationship with family members—especially your spouse.

A persistent and dedicated attitude is a great attribute. However, your persistence and dedication should *never* get to the point where it means you're ignoring your family duties. Believe me, doing so can only lead to problems. Let's face it, there's no way you can be an effective hunter if you're sitting on your stand and worrying about whether or not your marriage or your relationship with your girlfriend or boyfriend is going to survive.

So how do you go about ensuring your dedicated and persistent hunting attitude won't wind up costing you a spouse? Well, I'm afraid I don't have a remedy for each and every situation. I can, however, tell you what I've done to help keep things running smoothly in my household.

To begin with, I let my wife know well in advance where I'll be hunting and exactly how long I'll be gone. Then we sit down and figure out if my schedule is going to conflict with any family commitments. If so, we do what we have to do to remedy the situation.

Also, my wife has a job outside of our home. To help her out, I do as many chores around the house as possible. That's right, yours truly does housework. I cook, I clean, I wash dishes, I do laundry, I drive my kids to and from school and do a lot of other chores many men would consider beneath them. And I don't do these things simply because I'm trying to get on my wife's good-side. I do them because I believe our relationship is a two-way street.

Believe me, I've seen far too many relationships go down the tubes because the husband/boyfriend became completely obsessed with their hunting activities.

A strong and cooperative relationship with your spouse can be instrumental in retaining the proper mental outlook throughout the season.

Again, persistence and dedication are strong qualities for deer hunters. But so are responsibility and commitment to your family. Being a bit more understanding and helpful around the house really won't cost you a thing. Developing such an attitude can only make things better.

Set Your Standards High—And Keep Them There

The last aspect of keeping a proper mental outlook I want to talk about has do to with accepting the fact that there are going to be seasons when your tag will go unfilled. (And believe me, once you decide to raise your standards a bit, there are going to be quite a few "buck-less" seasons.) From past experiences, I can state that this might well be the toughest aspect of the mental side of trophy whitetail hunting.

Keeping the proper mental outlook means you can't let anything, not pressure from friends or peers or even the thought of ending the season with an 'open tag', force you into suddenly lowering your personal standards. Even at the last minute on the last day of the season you must remain true to the vows you made at the beginning of the season. And you can't let the fact that you went deerless undermine your positive outlook. When you're able to do this, then I'd say your mental state has been honed to a fine edge.

Greg's Proven Pointers

- Dedication and persistence are worthless if you have trouble attaining and then retaining the proper mental outlook.

- It's especially critical for bow-hunters to develop a positive and upbeat mental attitude.

- You can't let bad experiences from past hunts ruin future hunts. It's important to remember that there will always be another day.

- When dealing with mature bucks there's seldom such a thing as the perfect shot situation. Proper mental preparation will help you deal with rapidly changing conditions.

- Honing your mental edge also means developing an effective strategy for dealing with bouts of buck fever. For some, this just might be the most important aspect of mental conditioning.

- Above all, honing your mental edge means keeping a good balance in your life. Don't get so involved in the sport that your relationships with family and friends goes down the tubes.

CHAPTER THREE

Understanding Buck Core Areas

A great deal of the success I've enjoyed on trophy white-tailed deer can be linked directly to one factor—I've made it a point to gain a basic understanding of buck core areas.

I'm convinced that the majority of successful whitetail hunters would agree with me regarding the importance of finding and hunting buck core areas. I've talked with enough people who fit into this category to know the importance they place·on gaining familiarity with the bucks they plan on hunting. According to them, the best way of accomplishing this task is by finding out all they can about core areas.

No doubt just about everyone who is interested in hunting trophy whitetails has heard the term "core area" many times. But even though it's a very familiar term, I wonder just how many whitetail hunters really know what is meant when we speak of a buck's core area?

My concern stems from the fact that I've heard some definitions of core areas that were so far off the mark that they bordered on being ridiculous. For example, I recently watched a hunting video that featured a so-called "trophy whitetail expert." This guy was walking through the woods when he happened to find sev-eral antler rubs and a couple fresh scrapes. Looking into the camera, the guy explained, "These clusters of fresh buck sign are what experienced deer hunters often refer to as a core area." Wrong!

A couple years ago I was attending a large deer show in the upper Midwest. I decided to sit in on one of the seminars being held that day. The person giving the seminar was another supposed whitetail "expert." And in truth, this guy gave what

I thought was a pretty decent presentation. Unfortunately, he tipped his hand in regards to his knowledge when, at the end of his seminar, he was asked about buck core areas. "Core areas are those places that big bucks take estrous does during the rut," the featured speaker explained. "In fact, the rut is the only time you'll ever catch a big buck using one of his core areas." Whoa, very wrong!

Defining Core Areas

So what is a more accurate definition of buck core areas? Well, in the simplest terms, core areas are those places inhabited by whitetail bucks during non-breeding or non-stressful times. When they're not chasing receptive does or struggling to survive life-threatening situations or harsh elements, bucks will spend the majority of their time feeding, watering and traveling within the boundaries of an *established range*. According to people who *really* spend a lot of time chasing mature whitetails, this is the most accurate description of a core area.

Just how large is a core area? Well, as you might suspect, no two core areas are the exact same size. Many factors can dictate just how much acreage each individual buck will include in his core area. The single largest factor has to be the location of adequate bedding cover in relation to the location of preferred foods and, sometimes, watering spots.

Bucks that are able to find suitable daytime cover within spitting distance of primary food sources usually will establish relatively small core areas. Of course, the reverse is true in those situations in which bucks have to travel great distances from bedding to feeding areas. These deer most likely will have larger core areas. (Big woods whitetails fit into this category more so than farmland deer.)

For the most part, especially during late summer and early fall, whitetail bucks are pretty much homebodies. They spend the majority of their time bedding, traveling and feeding within their core areas. This all changes, though, once bachelor groups start breaking up.

Long-Distance Relocation

The heightened intensity of sparring matches and increased competition often are the main reasons for the breakup of bachelor groups. But while this might be common knowledge, there's a tidbit of information regarding this phenomenon that *is not* widely known.

It's my opinion that some hunters are under the impression that when bachelor group breakup occurs, dispersed bucks simply move a short distance and take up residency once more. While this is true in some cases, there are also those instances in which bucks will relocate quite some distance from their summer areas.

More and more in recent years I've listened to hunters talk about big bucks that were highly visible during the velvet stage but disappeared once the velvet was removed. At first, these guys suspected the bucks had simply gone underground—that they'd switched into their reclusive early fall lifestyles. However, when the inquisitive hunters expanded their scouting and observations a bit, they

I'm convinced that a thorough understanding of buck core areas can substantially increase your success rate on mature animals.

found that the bucks had relocated and established core areas some distance from where they originally had been living. Interestingly, some of these areas were miles from where they had lived during the velvet stage.

I'd be willing to bet a good sum of money that some of you have had experiences similar to what I've just described above. A big buck you've been watching suddenly disappears after shedding his velvet. While there's always a possibility he might have simply altered his habits and travel patterns, it's also entirely possible he has moved to another area altogether. This is especially possible if that buck happens to be a subordinate member of a bachelor group.

I know what some of you are thinking at this point. You could care less where a subordinate buck ends up relocating. But there's something terribly important to remember about the term "subordinate buck." Let's say you've got a bachelor group consisting of six bucks. The largest two in this group are bruisers scoring 160 or more Boone & Crockett points. The other four bucks are all in the 130- to 140-class range.

I would assume it's fairly obvious which of the above-mentioned bucks are most likely to relocate once the playful pushing and shoving of late-summer turns into more serious early-fall fighting. The four "smaller" bucks are going to take only so much abuse by the two stud bucks before they say 'adios' and move to less-stressful areas.

Now, even though the four 130- to 140-class deer are going to be looked upon as subordinates by the two larger members of the bachelor group, they most likely would be considered target animals by a lot of hunters, including me! As far as I'm concerned, it's going to be well worth my time to try and figure out exactly where these bucks wind up living after they relocate.

Core Areas Change with the Seasons

Another thing that hunters need to know is that bucks don't always stay within the same core area from late summer/early fall right on through to the late pre-rut period. Contrary to what many people believe, whitetail bucks will suddenly pull up stakes during the transition period (early-fall) and relocate to a completely different area. In most cases, this is where you'll find the majority of a buck's rub-lines and scrape-lines.

My good friend Tom Indrebo lives and hunts in trophy-rich Buffalo County, Wisconsin. Along with running a trophy-hunting operation called Bluff Country Outfitters, Tom has spent hundreds of hours observing and shooting footage of tremendous whitetail bucks for three popular deer videos. I have yet to meet the person that knows more about bucks and their core areas than Tom.

Tom agrees wholeheartedly with me on the important role that food and water seem to play in core-area location. "In my part of the country, bucks really seem to key on bean fields during the late summer and early fall," he told me.

"What I've seen would indicate that during late summer and early fall, big bucks usually live relatively close to their primary food sources. Occasionally, they'll

There are some cases where "subordinate bucks" could be good-sized animals. It pays to keep track of where these bucks relocate after bachelor groups break-up.

leave these core areas and make a swing through their favorite pre-rut areas, but then they quickly return to their summer core areas."

Tom's observations also have showed there's often a vast difference between summer core areas and pre-rut core areas. He told me that on a number of occasions, his partner and guide, Pat Reeve, filmed a tremendous buck just across the border in Minnesota. Because of the animal's size, Tom and Pat simply refer to the deer as the "Boonie Buck." "There were about 15 bucks in the bachelor group Pat was filming," Tom noted. "All these bucks were living and feeding in a relatively small area near a major ridge."

Interestingly, a couple of months later, on the opening day of Minnesota's gun season, Tom was shooting video footage of deer in a park that's closed to hunting. "I saw a number of different bucks that day, including a monster buck we've name 'Elvis,'" Tom remembered. "But even more surprising, I also saw and filmed the Boonie Buck in the park. He was roughly three miles from where Pat had filmed him earlier in the year." This is proof positive that bucks do indeed "change" core areas from late summer to late fall.

There's a problem here, of course. It can be quite a difficult task to find a big buck after he relocates. And finding that deer is only part of your problem. As my hunting partners and I have so painfully learned when hunting private land, there's a good chance that a big buck will relocate on property you don't have permission to hunt. What this means is that you'll have no choice but to go through the process of trying to obtain trespass rights on the buck's new stomping grounds.

Why Do Bucks Move?

There are many factors than can have a bearing on why a big buck suddenly decides to take up permanent residency in a new location. Conflicts with other bucks are near the top of the list. A shift in preferred foods is another reason for relocation. So is loss of habitat. However, pressure from humans also ranks near the top. As most serious deer hunters already know, mature whitetail bucks will take only so much harassment/interference from humans, and then they're gone.

So, just how much human pressure will a mature buck put up with before he decides to relocate? I'm afraid there's no cut-and-dried answer to that question. Too many variables can come into play, including individual buck temperament.

In most cases, it takes more than one or two obvious intrusions into a buck's home range or a single walk through his bedding area to force that deer to completely abandon his core area. Again, it's important to note that when a mature buck decides to pull up stakes, he might move some distance before once more establishing residency.

The Role of Water

I've already mentioned that water also can have a bearing on core-area location. Unfortunately, this fact isn't given enough consideration by hunters. Several times, especially during recent seasons, I've seen instances in which whitetails have completely abandoned established core areas and relocated, simply because those deer wanted to be closer to water.

A few years ago my good friend Gordon Whittington and I traveled to Manitoba for an early fall archery hunt for trophy whitetails. Prior to our arrival, guide Randy Bean had been keeping a close eye on the white-tailed deer living on the property we'd be hunting. From his observations, Randy had been able to ascertain that a good number of deer, including several shooter bucks, were spending the majority of their time on the south end of the acreage.

It's possible that big bucks could relocate to completely different core areas during the open season. Although there are many reasons why this might happen, hunting pressure is at the top of the list.

Using Randy's observations as a guideline, we spent the first couple of days hunting the south end of the property. It soon become clear, however, that the deer had moved. A bout of unseasonably hot weather apparently had dried up a couple of water holes, the only drinking spots in the south end of the area. Locating the next source of water, a small but deep creek, led us to discover that the deer had relocated to the opposite end of the property.

Hunters should be aware that it isn't always dry weather that influences bucks to relocate. Remember the tremendous flooding that occurred over much of the Midwestern United States during the summer of 1993? Well, I've talked to a lot of Midwestern deer hunters who live in areas that experienced extreme flooding in '93. Many of these guys told me the damage to their hunting areas, which obvi-

Buck Core Areas

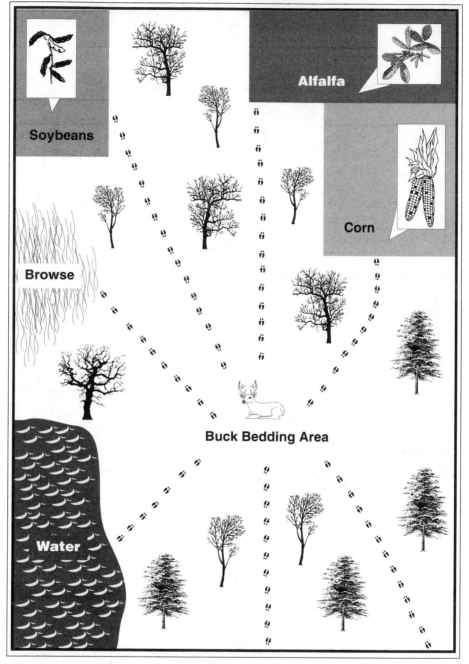

This is a rather simplistic example of what a buck core area looks like. It should be noted that the locations of bedding areas, food sources and water play a huge role in where bucks will establish their core areas. These factors also have a bearing on the core area size.

Buck Travel Routes
(Rub/Scrape-Lines)

ously was river bottom terrain, was so severe that it's doubtful if there ever again will be whitetails in places where they had lived for years. Still, those deer have to be living *somewhere*—it's just a matter of pinpointing their new core areas.

Staying at Home in the Big Woods

Throughout the years I've been paying close attention to such things, I've discovered a very interesting pattern. Mature bucks in big-woods environments seem more likely than farm-country bucks to live for years within the same core area.

The most obvious explanation I have for this is that, in most cases, big-woods deer aren't subjected to the same amount of human intrusion as their farmland cousins. So, once they discover a spot that can provide them with everything they need (adequate cover, safe travel corridors, relatively easy access to food, water, does, etc.), they stay put. In fact, biologists who have put radio-collars on mature big woods bucks have found that it takes a tremendous amount of snow to push these exceptional creatures out of their core areas and make them head for a deer yard. Often, this is why mature bucks are some of the first animals to die during a severe winter. By the time they decide to head for a yard, it's too late.

I should mention that with the ever-increasing logging practices being implemented these days in many heavily forested areas across North America, big woods bucks are surely bound to be relocating more often than before. Common sense should tell you that these wary creatures are not going to remain living in an area where all the trees have been mowed down.

I stated earlier that much of what takes place with regard to core areas could be dependent upon individual buck temperament. For instance, my brother and I have been hunting a certain big buck for five years now. Over the course of that time, we've picked up five shed antlers from the deer. Our observations of this animal show he's a minimum of eight years old—a true warrior!

Over the years we've studied the old buck, we've noticed something interesting about him. He doesn't show up on our farm until December. Usually, he'll then stay in the area all through the winter. (The past few years he has been highly visible during this time.) We never see him during the late summer or fall, even though, believe me, we spend a lot of time both observing and hunting this particular area.

Jeff and I are convinced the buck is living in a different core area(s) during the summer and fall months. Then, regardless of the severity of the winter, he relocates onto our property in December. Why? The answer to that question means dealing in a bit of speculation. We strongly suspect it's a combination of rather heavy gun-hunting pressure in outlying areas and the availability of preferred winter foods on our farm. Then again, maybe it's merely a pattern that was imprinted upon him when he was following his mama around during the very first year of his life.

My brother Jeff with a fine 12-point buck he took during a recent archery season. Jeff's knowledge of the buck's core area was instrumental in his success.

The Power of the Rut

Of the many reasons why a buck might suddenly vacate his core area, the rutting urge remains the strongest influence of all. Sometimes, the instinct to breed can lead bucks away from their home ranges for up to a month. Once the rut is over, however, and provided they've survived the rigors of breeding, safely evaded hunters and successfully dodged car bumpers, mature bucks will most likely head back to the core areas they used during the pre-rut period.

Once they are safely back in their familiar haunts, these bucks will most likely start traveling along the same routes they used during the pre-rut period. The one difference is that, at least for the first week or so, they are going to severely restrict their movements. Any wandering will be from bedding to feeding areas and then right back to bedding areas. And most of this movement will occur under the cover of darkness—at least during the initial stages of the post-rut. After a week or so, however, you can expect to see the same dawn/dusk movement patterns the bucks displayed earlier in the fall.

My best bow-killed buck to date was taken on Dec. 13, 1990, during Wisconsin's late-archery season. As anyone from this part of the world will attest, this definitely is the height of our post-rut period. Yet I shot the big non-typical from a stand on one of his favorite pre-rut travel routes.

Actually, I had previous knowledge that the buck had returned to his pre-rut core area. You see, while doing a big of late-season scouting, my brother Jeff discovered that several huge rubs had suddenly appeared on a rub-line I'd hunted earlier in the fall. The day after Jeff reported this to me, I put up my portable stand in a tree I'd hunted out of previously. An approaching winter storm then further assisted me in getting the monster buck to walk out in the open during legal shooting time.

Still, there are those times when my hunting partners and I have noticed a distinct change in core-area locations between the early and late archery seasons here in the upper-Midwest. This seems to hold especially true during those years when we're experiencing extremely cold weather and/or deer snows. Under such conditions, we've found that the deer are most likely to establish core areas in very close proximity to the most abundant supply of winter-type foods.

I've talked at length throughout this chapter about the possibility that some whitetail bucks establish more than one core area. However, it's important to remember that I'm referring to that time frame falling between late summer and early winter. Actually, it's entirely possible, and quite probable, that some whitetails have separate core areas for spring, summer, fall and winter. Again, food and cover dictate *where* deer live and *when* they'll be there.

I'm confident most good deer hunters realize that the key to consistent success is getting to know the animals they're hunting. As I've learned over the years, the best way of accomplishing this task is by taking the time to figure out where a certain big buck prefers to feed, water and bed, and the routes he's using to reach his destinations. In other words, it would be wise to gain an intimate understanding of buck core areas.

Greg's Proven Pointers

- Core areas are those places inhabited by bucks during non-stressful or non-breeding times.

- The term "subordinate buck" can be misleading: These deer could be considered target animals by many hunters. Pay attention to where these bucks end up after dispersal.

- Hunting pressure is a big reason a big buck will suddenly relocate to a completely different area during the open season.

- Big woods deer are more apt to establish larger core areas. I believe this is because, in most cases, it's a greater distance between preferred food sources.

- Provided a buck survives all the hazards associated with hunting season and the rut, he will usually return to the same core area he used during the pre-rut period. This can be valuable information for late-season hunters.

CHAPTER FOUR

Calling Bucks— The Right Way!

You probably don't need me to tell you that calling for whitetail bucks is a tremendously popular tactic. In fact, I seriously doubt there's one aspect of hunting for trophy whitetails that has received more attention in the past 10 years.

But to be honest, the attention that calling has garnered in recent years is well-deserved. As those who have had the unique opportunity will attest, there's nothing quite as exciting as calling-in and harvesting a monster buck. For that matter, just getting a buck—any buck—to respond to a bit of antler rattling and/or grunting can be an exhilarating experience.

For the skeptics who are reading this, let me assure you, calling can be a deadly tactic in nearly all regions of North America. I've been successful at calling in big bucks just about everywhere I've hunted. If you're thinking that big bucks can't be fooled with rattling antlers and grunt calls, think again. My biggest typical buck to date, a monster 13-point typical that gross-scores 180-3/8, was rattled-in.

Perhaps I should mention right off that this chapter isn't going to be as much about "how-to call" as it is about "what-not-to-do" when calling. It's my opinion that hunters who fail to call-in bucks are making some very basic mistakes. Unfortunately, unless these hunters are made aware of what those mistakes are, and given some idea of what to do different, they might never catch on.

Calling can be an effective strategy for taking mature bucks. I shot this Boone & Crockett 13-pointer after rattling him in at high noon!

Far too many hunters are under the impression that you can walk into the woods just anywhere and rattle-in a buck-wrong!

Calling from the Right Place

One of the biggest misconceptions of prospective callers is thinking that they can walk in the woods anywhere and call-in a buck. These individuals do what most sure-to-fail callers do. They spend the majority of their time calling from spots where, A) no buck is going to hear their calling efforts, or B) no buck in his right mind would consider approaching, even if he does hear the call.

Although this may sound extremely basic, to be effective at calling in bucks you first have to set up in a spot that will put you within hearing range of at least one antlered animal. Alas, if my personal observations in recent years are any indication, a lot of hunters are rattling and/or grunting from stand sites where even their best efforts aren't being heard.

Okay, so let's say you've done your homework and pinpointed an area where you know a couple of big bucks are living. Heck, you've actually seen the two antlered beauties on a number of occasions. Still, try as you might, you've been unable to get either one of the bucks to respond to your calling efforts. So what's the deal?

Remember what I said earlier about hunters calling from spots where no buck in his right mind would consider approaching? This is without a doubt the most common and costly mistake hunters make. Even though bucks may be hearing a hunter's best calling efforts, there's no way those deer are going to waltz in and investigate the sounds.

Here's an analogy that I think perfectly illustrates my point. Let's say you live in one of the larger cities in this country. There are certain places in those cities where you aren't safe to walk—*especially after dark*. Not only could such a venture lead to serious personal injury, it might well lead to your demise.

The remedy, however, is simple: To avoid getting into a situation that might cost you life or limb, you simply stay away from those parts of the city that are known to be dangerous. And you just can't let any form of enticement lure you into the area.

Okay, so let's say we have a mature whitetail buck that lives in a rather large woods. I'd be willing to bet there are places in that woods where the buck knows he shouldn't walk—*especially during daylight hours*. Not only could such a decision lead to serious injury, it could prove to be life-threatening.

But once again, the remedy is simple: To avoid getting into a situation that might well cost him life or limb, a mature whitetail buck is going to stay away from those parts of the woods that he knows are dangerous. And nothing, no amount of antler rattling and/or grunting, is going to entice him into those areas.

What this means is, even though a certain part of a woods might look good to you, that doesn't necessarily mean the resident bucks feel safe and secure walking there, especially during daylight hours. And lest you think otherwise, no amount of "perfect" calling will convince a mature buck that he should relax his guard and walk into such areas!

So how do you go about locating those spots where a big buck does feel comfortable moving about during daylight hours? Actually, it's relatively simple. You see, even though they may have thousands of acres of land within their core areas, mature whitetail bucks seldom use all of that land. In truth, big bucks often restrict the majority of their traveling to very select corridors. These select corridors are not established just anywhere either.

In most cases, the preferred travel lanes of mature bucks will be laid out along routes where those bucks feel the most safe and secure when walking about. To our benefit, these routes are usually quite clearly marked with a line of antler rubs. And these active buck rub-lines are the best places to attempt to call-in a whitetail.

I hasten to add, however, that setting-up just anywhere along an active rub-line won't necessarily ensure calling success. As many hunters know, mature bucks often hesitate to venture too far from their bedding areas in daylight. This remains true even if they hear the sounds of two bucks fighting or a series of challenging grunts coming from the direction of one of their primary travel routes. For this reason, you should attempt to place your stands as close as possible to buck bedding areas.

The Prime Time to Call

Hunters should also be aware that just as there are prime places from which to call, there also are prime times when bucks are more likely to respond to calling.

46

Bucks establish rub-lines along those routes they feel the most safe and secure using. You'll see more positive responses to your calling efforts if you're set up along an active rub-line.

My most successful calling times have been during the first hour of daylight in the morning and the last hour of legal shooting time in the afternoon.

Time of day isn't the only prerequisite to successful calling—the time of year also has a big bearing on calling success rates. Whitetail bucks are most likely to respond positively to rattling and grunting during the mid to late pre-rut period. To narrow it down even more, bucks will be *most* responsive—to rattling especially—during that three to five day period just prior to when the first does start coming into estrous.

Many hunters have told me they wait a certain number of minutes after getting on their stand before they go through their first calling sequence. As one guy told me recently, "I always wait a minimum of thirty minutes for things to settle down before I try some calling." Not a bad idea, but I believe my own theory on how long you should wait for things to settle down is more sound.

I don't wait a predetermined number of minutes before I begin calling. Rather, after getting settled in my stand, I pay attention to my surroundings. When the songbirds flit back into the area and start singing, when the woodpeckers return and start hammering away, when the squirrels climb back down to the ground and renew their search for acorns, I know the area has settled down. More importantly, any big bucks that might be bedded within earshot of my stand-sites also are confident that whatever threat might have existed earlier is now long gone.

The Calling Strategy

Once I feel confident things have returned to normal in the immediate area, I go through my first calling sequence. I like to start out by issuing three soft grunts on my grunt call. I call once to my right, once straight ahead and once to my left. Then I put away my grunt call, grab my bow and sit silently for several minutes.

If I don't see or hear anything after three to five minutes, I then go through a 30- to 45-second sequence of mock rubbing. The intensity of this mock rubbing is dictated solely by the time of season. During the early to mid pre-rut period the mock rubbing usually is more subtle and meant to make a listening buck curious. But from the mid pre-rut time on, I'll turn up the intensity of my mock rubbing substantially. At this time of year, I want a big buck to feel as though another buck is issuing a challenge.

There have been several occasions when a buck has come charging in upon hearing the mock rubbing. These experiences have taught me that it's wise to quickly and quietly put aside the antlers and get my bow in hand as soon as I've finishing the mock rubbing sequence.

If after a few minutes I detect no response to the mock rubbing, I'll set aside my bow and once again pick up the rattling antlers. I'll then go through my actual rattling sequence. This sequence will last 30 to 45 seconds. Again, the intensity of the rattling (the frequency and severity of the twisting and grinding of the antlers) is dictated *mainly* by the time of season. During the early to mid pre-rut I'll do a lot more "tickling" and less twisting and grinding. Also, I don't try for a lot of volume at this time of year.

From the mid to late pre-rut, however, my rattling sequences become much more "angry" and intense. I twist and grind the antlers together with quite a bit of force. It's my intent to produce as much volume as possible. Believe me, actual knock-down, drag-out buck fights are anything but quiet or half-hearted.

There's a good reason why I like to incorporate grunting, mock rubbing and rattling into my calling sequences. There is usually much more to buck fights than two antlered animals meeting in the woods, lowering their heads and going at it. In most cases, there's a good deal of posturing that goes on first. And when bucks posture, they often grunt (grunt call). Also, to avoid having to fight, both bucks are going to do all they can to intimidate the other. They often do this by scraping and/or rubbing (mock rubbing). But if posturing and intimidation doesn't work, then a fight is inevitable (rattling).

Knowing When *Not* to Call

Okay, let's say you take what you've read thus far in this chapter and apply it during the upcoming season. Lo and behold, you manage to call in a big buck. However, instead of charging right into bow range, the monster deer stops approximately 60 yards from your stand site and stares hard in your direction (this is a common occurrence). After a tense 30-second wait, you're convinced the buck isn't coming any closer. Now what?

Further calling when you have a buck at this range usually proves to be more damaging than helpful. My advice is to sit still and be quiet!

Well, if you're like many deer hunters I've talked with over the years, you're going make a very common and costly mistake. Instead of sitting motionless and quiet, you pick up your rattling antlers or dig out your grunt call and try to entice that big buck a bit closer. But while a bit of "tickling" with the antlers or a couple soft toots on the grunt call might seem to be the perfect ticket, most times it isn't. In fact, in most instances, instead of making the buck more curious, your additional calling efforts will make him instantly suspicious.

Look at it this way. Let's say you and your buddies walk out of "Joe's Cold Ones" and hear two guys going at it tooth and nail. I mean you can actually hear the two combatants punching, kicking, grunting and even farting. It's happening right there in front of you. The only problem is, they're nowhere to be seen. No matter how hard you try, you can't see the terrible fight that's supposedly going on just a couple of feet from you. Wouldn't you be just a bit suspicious that somebody is trying to pull something on you? After all, if it sounds like two guys are fighting under your nose—you should be able to see that fight, right?

This is basically the same scenario you'll run into if you attempt to entice a mature buck just a bit closer with some additional calling. Believe me, big bucks know when they are within sight of where a supposed fight has just occurred. If they hear the sounds of more fighting, or if they hear another buck grunting, they know they should see one or two bucks standing right in front of them.

I've found that the best strategy to employ when a buck stops outside your effective range is to just sit silent and wait. Hopefully, the buck's curiosity will get the best of him and he'll move in close enough for a shot. If you insist on trying to call him closer, his curiosity will evaporate and quickly be replaced by suspicion. With mature whitetails, suspicion is closely followed by fright.

Another important point: If a big buck turns to go, don't try any further calling. Sit quietly and let him walk away. If you've managed to dupe the deer once, there's a good chance you'll be able to fool him again on a future hunt. But only if don't you educate him to the fact that the sounds of two bucks fighting or a buck grunting is something suspicious.

What I'd suggest is to return to that same area in a couple of days and set up in a slightly different location. Also, use a slightly different calling routine than you used the first time. I've both seen and heard about this strategy working to bring in a buck that proved to be a bit call-shy the first time around.

Fooling the Circling Buck

There's another problem many hunters frequently encounter when calling: A big buck responds to the sounds of some calling, but before coming within bow range, he circles to the downwind side of the hunter's position. Eventually, the deer catches the hunter's odor, which ruins their chances of having the buck come any closer.

Believe it or not, I've discovered an effective way to deal with these circling bucks. Before climbing to my tree stand, I hang two 35mm film canisters stuffed with cotton on some underbrush, 15 to 20 yards from both sides of my stand site. I then squirt some pure buck urine scent in both canisters.

What's the reason for placing the scent canisters on either side of my stand site? Simple. Let's say a big buck responds to my rattling. But instead of coming straight in, the deer decides to circle downwind to check for danger. No need to panic. Before that buck ever hits my scent-stream, he's going to get downwind of the scent-canisters. In almost every instance where I've had this happen, the buck immediately turned and came walking in to investigate the odor, which resulted in a 15- to 20-yard shot. Even I don't miss many bowshots at that distance.

It's important to remember that when a big buck responds to your calling efforts, it means you've fooled his sense of hearing. But this doesn't necessarily mean he's going to come charging in. The real trick to getting a big buck within bow range is to fool *two* of his senses. As stated, you've already fooled his sense of hearing. And when he smells the buck urine (or maybe even a doe-in-heat

Calling in the Circling Buck

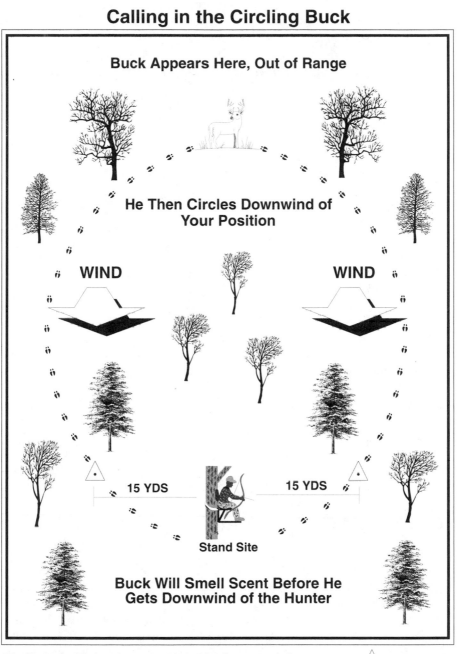

Buck Appears Here, Out of Range

He Then Circles Downwind of Your Position

WIND

WIND

15 YDS

15 YDS

Stand Site

Buck Will Smell Scent Before He Gets Downwind of the Hunter

Placing scent-filled canisters on either side of your stand site can be a great way to deal with bucks that respond to your calling, but then start circling before coming within range. These deer will smell the scent before they get downwind of your position.

△ Scent Canisters

Buck Travel Routes
(Rub/Scrape-Lines)

scent), you've also fooled his nose into thinking there is or has been another deer in the area. Any time you can dupe two of a buck's senses you're almost assured of getting a shot!

More Rattling Isn't Necessarily Better

Another important aspect of calling is how often you should rattle. I believe many hunters are under the impression that if a little is good, then more certainly must be better. That's far from the truth, however.

If full-fledged fights between mature bucks occurred as often as some so-called "experts" would have you believe, you wouldn't be able to walk through the woods during any stage of the rut without seeing or hearing a fight. How many actual buck fights have you seen or heard in the wild? I doubt most hunters have seen or heard even one!

Still not convinced that full-fledged fights between big bucks are rare? Well then, let me offer this. If big bucks fought as often and as intensely as some people think, it only stands to reason that each year a large number of monster bucks would get their antlers locked together in a deathly embrace. If this truly were the case, then you wouldn't be able to walk through the woods without tripping over the many sets of locked antlers lying around. Tell me, how many sets of locked antlers have you found?

I believe the two previous paragraphs help prove the point I'm trying to make: Fights between bucks—especially between big bucks—really are quite rare. So if mature bucks don't fight that often or that intensely, doesn't it stand to reason that they might get suspicious if they hear an intense "buck fight" every ten minutes or so?

Believe me, this is one of those cases where a little bit is good, but more is NOT better! In fact, throughout most of the pre-rut period, I usually go through a full rattling sequence only once every hour. Toward the very end of the pre-rut period, during that "magical" three to five day period I mentioned earlier, I may rattle every 30 minutes. But never more often than that.

Vary Your Calling Patterns

One other thing I should mention—I don't do everything exactly the same way each time I call. For instance, if I blow on my grunt call three times during my first calling sequence, I may blow on it only once the second time around. I'll also either shorten or lengthen my mock rubbing sequence. And if I rattled 30 to 45 seconds the first time, I might only rattle for 15 to 20 seconds the next time I call.

I never use the exact same calling sequence two times in a row. But I know this is yet another mistake many hunters make. They do the exact same things each and every time they call. Worse yet, all this calling is done from the same stand site. (Remember, far too many bow-hunters spend all their time on one stand.)

If you're under the impression that things like this are trivial and don't make a difference, you're terribly mistaken. First of all, no two buck fights sound exactly

Remember, no two buck fights sound exactly alike. Hence, each of your rattling sequences should be at least slightly different.

the same, nor does every fight last exactly the same amount of time. Second, every fight doesn't take place in exactly the same location. I seriously doubt if a mature buck is going to become curious when he hears the exact same calling routine, lasting the exact same amount of time and coming from the exact same place every day.

Contrary to what you might have heard or read, calling can be effective during the rut. The key is to pay attention to what's happening in your hunting areas.

Calling During the Rut

I've stressed that the late pre-rut period is the best of all times to try to call big bucks within range of your stand-sites. But that doesn't mean you should put away your rattling antlers or grunt calls once you see actual breeding activity occurring. As I've learned in recent years, calling can be quite effective during this part of the season also.

I stated earlier that rattling was responsible for my bagging the largest typical whitetail I've taken to date. Most interestingly, that particular hunt occurred during the peak of the rut. What prompted me to try some rattling at a time when the tactic normally isn't very effective? Easy. In the three days prior to my killing the Boone & Crockett-class deer, I'd seen several big bucks cruising around in the area searching for hot does. As I can personally attest, anytime big bucks are "between does," they're extremely susceptible to a bit of calling.

The key to knowing when you might want to try to call in a rutting buck is to pay attention to what's going on in your hunting areas. If you see big bucks cruising around *all by themselves*, and you're positive they aren't on the trail of a hot doe, it might be time to try some calling.

Personally, I prefer to rattle when I'm attempting to call in cruising bucks I haven't actually seen. However, I usually won't use my rattling antlers if I have a cruising buck within sight (unless that deer is a good distance away). Most times when I have a buck in sight, I'll blow softly on my grunt call a couple times in an attempt to entice him within range.

Maybe you're thinking that what I've just said is a direct contradiction to what I stressed earlier about *not* calling when you have a buck in sight. However, I was talking earlier about bucks that were in a pre-rut mode. I'm talking here about bucks that are displaying full-rut behavior. There's a vast difference. A buck that might have been overly suspicious and extra-cautious earlier in the season might come charging in to some rattling or grunting during the rut.

Lastly, it's important to remember that calling will only be efffective on rutting bucks that aren't being sidetracked in any way by an estrous doe. I think a bit of common sense will tell you that a big buck isn't going to abandon one hot doe just to investigate the sounds of two bucks that *might* be fighting over another hot doe. Nor will he leave the trail of a hot doe to check out what *might* be some tending grunts. In truth, the best strategy to employ when you see a buck trailing, chasing or tending a hot doe is to sit quietly and hope the doe leads her suitor within range of your stand.

So maybe you're one of the many deer hunters who has been unsuccessful at calling-in big bucks. And maybe you believe your lack of calling success is because the whitetails in your part of the world just won't respond to rattling antlers or grunt calls. Could be. However, I'm more apt to believe that your lack of success is due more to the fact that you've been making some basic, yet common mistakes.

I'm confident that if you employ some of the strategies I've outlined in this chapter, you'll see an eventual rise in your calling success rates. The way I look at it, if you've had no luck at calling in bucks in the past, what have you got to lose?

Greg's Proven Pointers

- Even the most mature bucks can occasionally be duped by a bit of calling—provided it's done right!

- The Number One mistake prospective callers make is that they call from totally unproductive spots.

- Rub-lines are established along those routes that bucks feel the most safe and secure using. Obviously, these are some of the best places from which to try and call in a big buck.

- Another big mistake hunters make is to continue calling once they have a buck within sight. My advice is to sit still and be quiet. Let the buck's natural cuiosity get the best of him.

- The common belief when calling is that if a little bit is good, then more must be better. Wrong! Rattling antlers and/or grunt calls should be used sparingly.

- Calling during the rut can be effective. However, don't expect that you'll be able to call a buck away from a "hot" doe. Bucks that are on the prowl, looking for a prospective mate, can be very susceptible to calling.

CHAPTER FIVE

In-Season Scouting

Recently, I was giving a seminar to a large group of deer hunters. The subject for my talk dealt with using off-season scouting as a means for becoming more familiar with your hunting areas.

Anyway, during the question-and-answer period that followed my seminar, one hunter confronted me with a rather interesting situation. "I didn't get a lot of free time during the off-season this past year, but the free time I did get was spent scouting the one area I planned on hunting most," he told me. "Even with the limited time I had, I really thought I'd done a pretty thorough job. In fact, I was confident I had everything figured out. But then I ran into a bit of problem."

The fellow went on to say that some time during the middle of the season the area he was hunting suddenly went "dead." The deer simply vanished. Making matters worse was the fact that the guy didn't know much about in-season scouting. Because of this, he admitted that he probably spent more time doing things wrong than vice-versa. "Every time I found an area that showed a lot of promise, I'd do some scouting and then select and prepare a stand site," he stated. "But somehow, I must have been alerting the deer. They seemed to know exactly where my stands were located. Of course, they'd avoid those areas like the plague. Eventually I'd have to walk around and try to find another good stand site. Then the whole situation would repeat itself. Can you tell me what I was doing wrong?"

Much has been written about the importance of spring and pre-season scouting. Admittedly, I'm one writer who has certainly expounded on the importance of spending time in the woods during the off-season. So much so, in fact, that I've

occasionally ignored how critical it is to be proficient at dealing with rapidly changing conditions during the open season. However, because of some experiences my
hunting partners and I have had recently, the importance of being able to first locate
and then take a big buck during the open season has really hit home for me.

Changing Techniques With the Season

There is a world of difference between the way you approach pre-season and
in-season scouting for trophy bucks. For one thing, you're dealing with animals
that are living under quite different, but very influential, conditions. During the
pre-season, the Number One concern of the deer herd is getting a belly full of
nutritious food every day. Across most of the white-tailed deer's range, natural
predation is relatively non-existent. This means that during the pre-season period
the deer, although always alert, retain a relatively calm demeanor.

Once hunting seasons open, however, this demeanor changes immediately.
Sudden human presence in areas that saw no human activity in previous months
can have a profound effect on the behavior of white-tailed deer. This is true even
if the humans who "invade" an area are doing so in search of small game and/or
upland birds. But if these humans suddenly begin concentrating their hunting
efforts solely on deer, behavior patterns change even more. This is why you must
apply different techniques during in-season scouting missions.

But let's back up and talk about scouting at other times of the year, namely the
post-season and spring periods. Let's assume that you spent many hours in the
woods during the past winter and spring figuring out the travel patterns and habits
of a monster buck you're now hunting. You thought you had the big boy pegged.
His rub-lines were as obvious as a bug on the end of your nose. On top of that, you
were able to find both of his shed antlers during a spring scouting trip, so there's no
doubt he survived last year's hunting season and the harsh winter months.

You were careful to take everything into consideration regarding how to
effectively hunt the trophy deer. In fact, you spent so much time and effort on
this one deer, you didn't really have any time left to scout other areas. Still, that
wasn't much of a concern because you figured it was just a matter of time before
you'd be rewarded with a chance at "your" buck.

Initially, things were going quite well. You even saw the big buck on a couple
of occasions. But then almost overnight, something happens that really throws a
kink in your game plan. The area you spent so many hours studying and getting
to know so intimately suddenly has gone cold. For one thing, there's no fresh
sign anywhere in the vicinity of your stand site. On top of this, deer sightings
have just about ceased. Even more disturbing is the fact that less than half the
season remains.

Faced with the prospect of finding a new hunting area and getting to know
that area well enough to put yourself into position to kill a big buck can leave you
with an overwhelming feeling of doubt. Almost everything you've ever read

Because of the "minimal disturbance factor," there's a world of difference between how in-season and off-season scouting should be conducted.

regarding scouting your hunting areas dealt mainly with the proper steps to take during the off-season. But here it is the middle of the season and you're suddenly without a hot hunting area. Now what?

I once spent almost the entire early archery season in Wisconsin trying to pattern a certain big buck. Each time I thought I had the deer figured out, something would happen to make him alter his travel routes. The first time, it was the fact that a preferred food source suddenly came into season. The second time, his behavior changed slightly because of pre-rut conditions. Just when I figured out his pre-rut travel patterns, the buck got heavily involved in the breeding ritual. Eventually, because of some successful in-season scouting, I was able to get the big buck within fifteen yards of my tree stand. As they say, the rest is history.

Look for the Fresh Rubs

The secret of my harvesting that big buck lay in having a basic understanding of how to effectively scout during the open season. In this particular case, the primary key to success were the fresh rubs that continued to appear almost daily. Some of these rubs were found on my walks into and out of my hunting area. I also spotted a couple right from my tree stand.

The rubs were vitally important in determining some key factors. To begin with, I knew the buck was still alive. In addition, I knew he was at least occasionally frequenting the area. Lastly, by following a couple of his rub-lines I got a good idea of where he was feeding and also where he was hiding out during the day.

Most importantly, however, one of his rub-lines led me to discover where a good number of antlerless deer were living. I knew it would be just a matter of time before the big buck showed up in that area once the rut kicked into high gear. The morning I shot him, he had his nose to the ground and was quite obviously tracking a hot doe that had passed through before I'd climbed into my tree.

I mentioned that antler rubs played a large role in my being able to keep track of this buck. The fact that it's in their nature to leave behind rub-evidence is, in my opinion, the Number One downfall of whitetail bucks. From the minute they shed their velvet, not a day goes by that a buck doesn't rub his antlers on something. To our benefit, this rubbing activity only increases as the rut draws nearer.

Take it from someone who extensively studied this aspect of whitetail buck behavior—these animals usually leave clear indication of where they prefer to walk. Even if you somehow lose track of a big buck early in the season, or if you're forced to look for a different hunting area, there's no reason to fret. Periodic and careful scouting trips should enable you to pinpoint the exact location of a buck's travel routes. You can do this by finding and following fresh rub-lines.

Using Scrapes and Runways

Scrapes are another good indicator that a buck is still alive and occupying a specific area. Although scrapes may be abandoned during the actual breeding period, they are checked and freshened often during the lengthy pre-rut period. (They might also be reopened and run again during the post-rut period.)

Kicking leaves into scrapes and then checking them a couple of times a day to see if they've been cleaned out can tell you a couple of things. Again, you'll be able to determine if a certain buck is still in the area. More importantly, you might be able to establish the sort of a schedule a buck is using to run his scrape-line.

A word of caution here: If you're going to monkey around near scrapes, I'd suggest wearing your odorless hunting clothes. It's also best to wear rubber boots. This is especially important when dealing with mature animals. Make sure to keep

Antler rubs are the best scouting aid hunters have at their disposal. Fresh rubs and rub-lines can help you pinpoint hubs of buck activity and preferred travel routes.

Checking runways periodically throughout the season can keep you up-to-date on where deer are feeding and traveling.

your hands off the overhanging, or "licking," branch, as it's commonly known. (I can't tell you the number of times I've seen hunters grab onto licking branches.)

Checking runways daily can also be an effective way of determining deer activity in an area. If you have to, rake the trail clean of leaves and debris in select spots on two or three different runways. Then, if the ground is too hard or dry to show tracks, loosen up the soil along about a two-foot stretch. This should be adequate to show you exactly what is traveling on the runways.

If you're hunting a truly big deer, you should have no trouble distinguishing his tracks from those of the does, fawns and small bucks that might walk down the same runways. In fact, a few years ago I kept track of a big buck throughout the entire archery season just from occasionally finding his track. I was unable to narrow down the buck's travel pattern during the early fall months, but it was a different story later, during our gun season. Thanks to my continued in-season scouting efforts, I was able to finally put all the pieces of the puzzle together and get my stand placed in the right location. I shot the thick-bodied 8-pointer as he exited his bedding area late in the afternoon on the third day of the season.

I'm sure some hunters are under the impression that it's impossible to hunt and scout at the same time. I suppose this is true to a degree. You see, I know a number of deer hunters who take books up into their tree stands with them to help pass the time. Still others I've talked with told me they strap themselves to the tree and sleep through the "worthless times."

Observation has been a key ingredient to my success on mature bucks. Simply put, I pay attention to my surroundings when I'm on my stand.

This is one of the biggest reasons a lot of hunters never are able to get into that "perfect" position. They simply don't pay attention to what's going on around them while they're occupying their stands. I can't tell you the number of times I've observed buck activity in an area just slightly away from my stand site. I can tell you, however, that if I had been reading a book or, worse yet, sleeping, many of those bucks would have slipped by undetected. That's because most of them were only visible for a few seconds and passed by without making a sound (which is a trait common to big bucks). I wouldn't have seen them at all had I not been alert and observant.

Move Your Stand for Success

There's something else I should mention. A lot of hunters I've talked with in recent years have told me they absolute refuse to move their stands. As one guy told me this past year, "I don't like to be jumping around all over the place. Once I get my tree stands in place, I stay put. If a big buck walks by just out of range, I consider it bad luck. I figure it's only a matter of time before he walks by within range."

This guy's train of thought might be right on the money. Maybe a big buck he's seen in the distance will eventually walk by within range. But personally, I'm of the opinion that he could be in for quite a wait. As my hunting partners and I have learned, mature whitetails have the uncanny ability to figure out exactly where a stand has been placed. Often, they'll adjust their travel patterns just enough to bypass those spots.

Obviously, you don't want to be "jumping around all over the place" or creating any more disturbance in your hunting areas than needed. But if you actually witness a big buck walking through a certain spot, I feel strongly that it's well worth your time to do some snooping around in that spot. There have been many cases where doing just this has put me in position to eventually harvest a deer I saw walk by just out of range.

I guess I should add that you shouldn't use your stands purely as buck observation posts. In truth, you should pay attention to all deer activity around your stand sites. Often, your observations can be the final determining factor in whether or not it might be time to move on to another area.

This is a very important point. I'm convinced that far too many deer hunters suffer through periods of low success rates simply because they spend the majority of their time hunting in "dead" areas. It only stands to reason; if you spend six or eight hours a day on your stand on several different occasions and notice that all deer activity in the area has come to a standstill, it's definitely time to relocate.

Debunking Bedding Myths

Being successful at harvesting mature bucks often hinges on setting up close to where deer sleep. But if what we've been taught over the years is true, we must be extremely careful to never bump a big buck from his bedding area. As many trophy whitetail experts have assured us, even one close encounter with a bedded buck can be enough to force that deer to relocate—right?

Not necessarily. As my hunting partners and I have found in recent years, running a big buck out of his bedding area one time during the open season isn't quite as big a no-no as we once believed. In fact, we've found that this is the best of all ways to find out *exactly* where a big buck is hiding out during daylight hours. We'll walk around in his core area until we actually jump him from his bed.

If you're still convinced that wandering through buck bedding areas during the open season is strictly taboo, let me tell you this. Some of the bedded bucks we've jumped merely circled around after we left and came right back to lay in the exact same spot where they had originally been bedded. Obviously, these deer felt very comfortable in that spot—and they weren't going to let one intrusion change their minds!

There are some basic guidelines hunters should follow when attempting to find buck bedding areas during the open season. First, instead of sneaking around the woods and acting in a predatory manner, walk along at a fairly good clip. Second, if you manage to jump a buck from his bed, do some quick looking around and then vacate the area. And last but most important, after you've determined where a buck is bedding, don't walk through that spot again. While you may get away with running a buck from his bedding area once, repeated intrusions may indeed force him to bed elsewhere.

Walking through buck bedding areas during the open season isn't as big a "no-no" as some hunters would believe—provided you employ the proper approach.

No Time for Lounging

Several seasons back I came up with a very effective in-season scouting tactic that has served me well on a number of occasions. In that particular year, I killed my buck very early in the season. But instead of lounging around for the rest of the season (which is the normal practice of many hunters), I continued to poke and prod in the woods.

Interestingly, by the end of the season I had learned the whereabouts of several big bucks. More importantly, I was able to determine what parts of their ranges these deer were using and what times of the year they would be there. It only stood to reason that, provided those bucks survived, they would be back in the same places, doing the same things the following year. To make a long story short, I can tell you that one of those big bucks did survive. I was able to score on him the next season mainly because of what I'd learned during the previous open season.

Remember, the normal behavior patterns of any big buck will change dramatically when confronted with even moderate amounts of hunting pressure. The absolute best time to study this behavior is right as it's happening. So if you're fortunate and happen to fill your tag early in the season, don't be in such a hurry to put away your hunting clothes. Instead, return to the woods and attempt to figure out how other big bucks are managing to evade local hunters. Often, this is the only way to accurately predict what a big buck will do when he's faced with a bit of pressure. I know for sure it's the absolute best way!

This strategy doesn't just apply to bow-hunters either. Believe me, if a mature buck finds a place that offers him safety and solitude from the many gun-hunters tramping through the woods, he's not likely to forget about that place. If you can find out where this place is, you can be there waiting for him when he attempts to reach it next season. Or you might be able to implement a plan that will allow you and your buddies to push the hiding buck out of seclusion and past a waiting gun.

If you're currently spending a lot of time scouting your hunting areas in the off-season, continue to do so. Trust me, it can do nothing but help. But if you don't get to scout any other time during the year, or if you've been unable to finalize the findings from your pre-season scouting endeavors, or if your favorite hunting spots suddenly go cold, then it's time to do some in-season scouting.

As I've pointed out in this chapter, if done right, in-season scouting can go a long way toward helping you locate and then harvest a big buck. But if done wrong, scouting during the open season can have disastrous results. I guess the best advice regarding in-season scouting is to be careful and use some common sense. If you follow these two guidelines I'm confident you'll eventually find your own "in-season rhythm."

Greg's Proven Pointers

- In-season scouting has to be conducted in a much different manner than off-season scouting.

- One of the biggest keys to effective in-season scouting is learning how to decipher bits of buck sign, like antler rubs and rub-lines.

- Clearing leaves and debris from small stretches of runways and then periodically checking those spots is a great way to keep up-to-date on deer activity.

- Observation is another effective in-season scouting tool. Don't go to sleep or read a book on your stand while your waiting for "prime-time."

- Don't abandon the woods just because you've filled your tag. Continue to scout both the areas you're currently hunting and several areas you suspect migh have potential for future hunts.

CHAPTER SIX

Post- Season Scouting

I've had the pleasure of meeting, and even hunting with, some of the most successful trophy white-tailed deer hunters in North America. I guess what has impressed me most about these individuals is their approach to the sport. All of them have told me they spend hundreds of hours devising dependable and effective game plans for dealing with each individual animal they're pursuing.

You can tell just by talking to highly successful big buck hunters that everything has to be done to exact specifications. These great hunters know that in many instances they might get only one chance at a trophy deer. As one of them told me, "In almost every case, being able to harvest a certain big buck is directly dependent on all things going right the very first time I see that deer. I'm afraid this doesn't leave much margin for error." Amen to that!

I agree wholeheartedly that developing a sound game plan is a prime prerequisite for becoming consistently successful at taking mature whitetail bucks. We often get only one chance to make everything come together. Wouldn't it be nice if we were completely confident that one chance could mean the demise of a certain trophy buck we've been chasing?

The best hunters will tell you that thoroughly scouting your hunting areas is a big step in the right direction. And this means scouting at *all* times of the year. Personally, I've found that scouting during the post season period can go a long way toward establishing the confidence we need to become better deer hunters.

A wealth of information concerning spring and pre-season scouting can be found on the pages of almost every hunting magazine being published today. Yet, for all the scouting articles that appear in print, it's remarkable how little has

Often we'll get only one chance at a big buck we've singled out, but there are things we can do to increase our chances for success on that one encounter.

been written about post-season scouting. Maybe this is why so few hunters venture into their favorite hunting areas immediately after the season has closed.

I've already mentioned in previous chapters that I get the opportunity to talk to hundreds of deer hunters each year. Although I've learned much from these talks, one thing stands out above all else: There are a lot hunters who don't realize the importance of thoroughly scouting their hunting areas and the animals they're pursuing. Even fewer of these hunters understand just how beneficial post-season scouting can be. Could it be that a lack of familiarity with the animals and places you hunt is the main reason you're not able to kill a certain big buck you've been pursuing?

What is it about returning to the woods immediately after the season closes that turns people off? If my talks with hunters are any indication, it's because they think that scouting at this time of year is a complete waste of time. One hunter probably summed it up best when he told me that, "It just doesn't feel right to be walking around in my hunting areas during the post-season. Besides, I don't see where anything I learn at this time of year will help me next season."

Obviously, a lot of hunters simply aren't aware of the value of post-season scouting. In their defense, however, I think this is only because they've never tried it. As I've learned, most people find it hard to equate success with an unknown entity.

I find the post-season to be one of the most enjoyable and informative times of the year. This is especially true if you're fortunate enough to live or hunt in a

Although not a requirement, snow cover can be a great aid when attempting to evaluate the potential of a targeted area.

part of the country that normally experiences any kind of a snow cover. Snow is not only a great aid when searching for buck sign, you can sometimes even tell you just how fresh that sign is. To hunters like me who spend a lot of time chasing certain bucks, this is valuable information.

Fresh rubs (easily identifiable if bark from the rub tree is laying on top of a recent snowfall), tracks, scrapes and visual sightings can all be used to determine the status of the remaining buck population. Certainly the absence of one or more of these clues doesn't necessarily mean all the bucks in your hunting area have been killed off. However, the presence of fresh rubs, for example, positively indicates that some bucks survived. This gives you a starting point for determining possible future hunting areas.

For those of you who live and hunt in areas that receive little or no snow, the task of post-season scouting, while certainly more difficult, is not impossible. You simply have to get into the woods immediately after the close of your deer seasons and then stay in the woods for as long as it takes to do a thorough scouting job.

Sure, warm weather whitetail hunters may not have snow to aid them in their search for fresh sign, but they do get an extended amount of time for post-season scouting. I'd love to have that luxury. More times than not, our post-season scouting is cut short because snow depths get to the point where it becomes impossible to walk around.

Most times, I'll start my post-season scouting several weeks after the close of our gun-deer season (sometime in mid-December). By that time, most of the bucks have relaxed from the pressures of being kicked around day after day, which means they'll be back using the same travel routes and patterns they used earlier in the fall, during the pre-rut period.

Focus on Food Sources

Usually, I concentrate post-season scouting around known food sources. Remember, in areas where harsh winters are a possibility, it's imperative that big bucks quickly replenish the valuable body-fat they depleted while chasing does and evading hunters. This means they're going to "get back on their feed" as soon as the rut ends.

Even though the majority of this feeding activity may be occurring after dark, bucks are still going to leave evidence of their presence. Again, rubs, scrapes and big tracks found in and around food sources can all be indicators of buck presence.

Regardless of what the food source might be, if a big buck has been visiting the feeding area for any length of time, he will have established safe approach and exit routes to and from the spot. And the best way to figure out where these routes are is by first locating and then following active rub-lines.

How do I tell if a certain rub-line is being used in the morning or evening? Actually, it's quite simple. Rubs that were made as a buck walked to a feeding area usually will face in the direction of his bedding area. Just the opposite is generally true of the rubs a buck makes as he travels back to his bedding area. These rubs will be on the side of the tree that faces the food source. So a good rule of thumb to remember regarding rub-lines is this: *In most cases,* rubs will face away from a buck's actual line of travel.

Once I find an active rub-line, I attempt to follow it from the food source all the way to the buck's bedding area. But anytime I'm following an active rub-line, I'm also paying close attention to my surroundings. What I'm looking for are sites I might want to use as ambush points in the future. Hopefully, I can find a spot for my tree stand somewhere very close to where the buck is hiding out during the day

The Best Time to Find Bedding Sites

I can't think of a better time than the post-season period for hunters to attempt to pinpoint the exact location of buck bedding areas. In fact, this is my top priority at this time of year. By finding out everything I can about a big buck's favorite hiding spot now, I'm better able to figure out ways to effectively hunt him next season.

Your Number One goal during the post-season period is finding the location of buck bedding areas. Such information can prove invaluable during future seasons.

Following active rub-lines and/or often-used buck runways back away from feeding areas can be a good way to find bedding areas. I've also been able to locate bedding areas simply by using a bit of common sense and allowing my gut-feelings take over. Logic dictates that big bucks will establish bedding areas only in those places that offer them solitude, security and avenues for safe escape. There are only so many places like this in any woods.

To answer a question I'm often asked, yes, I do walk right through any spot I suspect might be holding a bedded buck. There's good reason for my behavior: I want to know for sure if a buck is bedding in that spot. As far as I know, the *only* way to be 100-percent positive is by actually jumping that deer right out of his bed.

So maybe you're one of those deer hunters who thinks you should *never* run a big buck out of his bedding area. Well, let me tell you this. My hunting partners and I have not seen a single instance where disturbing a big buck's bedding area once—especially during the post-season—has had a negative effect on our success rates. In fact, just the opposite is true. The majority of our big buck success is directly attributable to the fact that we knew exactly where those deer were bedding. Most times that information came about by actually jumping bucks from their beds.

Something else for you skeptics to keep in mind—remember, this is the post-season! The next open hunting season is many months away. What this means is that any bedded buck you bump now is going to have a lot of time to forget about the ordeal.

I mentioned earlier that I usually don't start my post-season scouting until several weeks after our gun-season closes. However, there have been times when I've returned to the woods immediately after the close of the season. Let's say a big buck has given me the slip during the gun-season. Because I'm always curious about such things, I want to figure out how that deer was able to evade me. And I've found the best way to do this is by thoroughly scouting the animal *while he's still in his strict survival patterns*.

By getting out in the woods immediately after the gun-season closes, I'll be able to study a buck under conditions that are very similar to those of the open season. You see, a deer has no idea exactly what day the season ends. Obviously, a big buck is going to stay in his survival patterns for quite a while after all the hunters have left the woods. Figure out what these patterns are and you could be a big step ahead of that buck when he pulls the same cute stunts on you next fall! (This tactic works equally well on both big country whitetails and farmland deer.)

I'll also walk right through any spot I suspect a big buck(s) might be using for a bedding area. Again, it's my intent to try to jump a buck out of his bed. In most instances when jumped, a buck will use one of his preferred escape routes. I pay close attention to exactly where these escape routes are located. During the next deer season I might just make a small, well organized "push" through the buck's bedding area. Of course, I will have posted a couple of my partners along the escape routes we've actually seen the buck use. If done right, this tactic can work to perfection.

Several years ago, I killed a dandy buck during our gun season here in Wisconsin. I had hunted that deer for a number of days without much success. Initially, I was trying to kill him by setting up in known feeding/breeding areas. Although I knew he was spending a lot of time in these spots, it soon became apparent the buck was doing so under the cover of darkness.

Eventually, I placed my stand at the very edge of what I strongly suspected was the buck's bedding area. Guess what? I'd discovered the spot while on a post-season scouting trip the year before. Daylight was fading fast when the buck finally made his appearance. After one well paced shot, the big deer was mine.

This only reinforces the point I've been stressing. Because so much big buck activity is going to be nearly nocturnal, locating bedding areas and establishing stand sites on the edges of these areas often is crucial to hunter success rates. There's no doubt in my mind this big deer would have continued to evade me had I not known about the bedding area. Just how close was I set up to where he was actually sleeping? Well, I doubt the heavy-beamed 8-pointer had taken more than 10 steps from his bed when I shot him.

This sort of behavior often is the norm for mature whitetails. With the ever-increasing pressure that's being put on them, big bucks seldom arrive at feeding areas or even travel along their rub-lines during legal shooting hours. However, they do display a distinct tendency to wander around near their bedding areas during legal shooting time.

This buck fell victim to a strategically placed bedding area stand. I located this bedding area during a post-season scouting trip the previous year.

Look for Shed Antlers

The best way to determine if a big buck made it through the previous season and the winter is by finding one or both of his shed antlers. You can look at huge rubs and scrapes from the year before and only hope the deer that made them is still around. But when you find a fresh shed, it's a safe bet the buck who lost that antler is alive and well and out there to be pursued in the upcoming season.

My hunting partners and I have picked up hundreds of shed antlers over the past 10 years. The remarkable thing about this is we're finding the majority of these antlers in some of the lowest deer density areas in the state of Wisconsin. Because of that fact, we've been accused of getting our antlers from deer kept in pens. But believe me, all of our antlers have come from wild deer.

Searching for shed antlers is best done in the spring immediately after the snow melts. Although this chapter was meant to deal mostly with post-season scouting, I feel strongly that finding shed antlers can be extremely crucial for being able to put together all the pieces of the puzzle.

For instance, while on a post-season scouting trip some years back, I located the home core area of what I believed was a huge whitetail buck. His consistently large rubs made me suspect that the deer was far above average, yet I wanted to be sure before wasting valuable time hunting him. On a return trip to the area in the spring, I found the buck's matched set of shed antlers. He was close to a B&C size animal. Now I had all the evidence I needed to justify spending a lot of time pursuing him.

To be successful at finding sheds, you must have at least some basic knowledge of where a number of deer spent the winter months. You can even do this from your vehicle. Drive through your hunting areas and make a note of the places where there appears to be a lot of concentrated deer activity. Visual sightings of groups of deer and "packed" runways are a couple of tip-offs. Also, you might want to talk to some of the local people and see if there are any deer feeding programs in the locale. This practice is getting more and more popular in the northern tier of states.

When you find areas where deer are wintering, there's really no need to do any leg work yet. You're much better off waiting until the snow has melted completely or is at a depth where you'll be able to see an antler sticking through whatever snow cover is left. But be advised it takes surprisingly little snow to hide a shed antler.

We find 60 to 70 percent of our shed antlers in bedding areas. In the winter months, especially during severely cold weather, whitetails decrease their movements by as much as 50 percent. They're able to get by with about 30 percent less food this way. It's obvious to see why we find so many of our sheds in bedding areas. The bucks are spending a lot of time here. The rest of the shed antlers we find are picked up on the trails going to and from feeding areas or right in the food sources themselves.

Finding shed antlers gives you a reliable way of evaluating both the quality and the quantity of the bucks in your hunting area.

The Right Way to Find Sheds

You might think a big, record book class shed antler laying on the forest floor would stick out like a thumb, right? Well, for the most part, you'd be wrong. The natural camouflage of antlers can make them extremely hard to find. Walking through the woods at a brisk pace glancing casually here and there is not the way to go about searching for sheds. Forget the idea that you'll be able to spot a big shed antler out of the corner of your eye. It very rarely happens that way. You'd be much better off to go about searching for antlers the same way you'd still-hunt for deer.

What I do is take two or three steps, stop and look around. I repeat this procedure all the way through any area that shows a lot of past winter deer activity. Brush that has been heavily browsed on and runways "muddied" from concentrated piles of deer droppings are a couple of indicators that an area experienced heavy deer use during the winter months.

Often, I've stood in one spot carefully scrutinizing the ground around me when all of a sudden I'll spot an antler. It may be laying in a place I had already searched, but I had overlooked it. Usually, this happens when I'm merely scanning an area instead of looking it over closely. Normally, I try to limit my searching to about a 15- to 20-foot radius of where I'm standing. This is about as far as I can see anyway in the spots where I find most of my sheds. Thick brush makes it impossible to see any further than that.

Finding your first shed antler can be quite a thrill for a hard-core whitetail fanatic. However, when you pick up your first set of matched antlers, you'll know what real excitement is. If you're fortunate enough to find a really big antler, I'd strongly suggest scouring the immediate area closely for the match. A buck with a heavy set of antlers usually will not go too far after losing one side of his rack before he'll attempt to kick or rub the other antler free. This may be because the buck feels slightly off balance with only one large antler on his head.

I know that by the time the post-season period rolls around, many people are burned-out on hunting and scouting. But you don't have to be in the woods and fields specifically for the purpose of doing some post-season scouting. Maybe you can couple your scouting with another activity like small-game or bird hunting. I'm not afraid to admit that I actually found one of my best farmland bow hunting stands while I was chasing after a fox. I'll also admit that I've found some big woods deer hunting hot spots while participating in hound hunts for bobcats and coyotes.

The trick is to learn to keep your eyes open for deer sign even when you're in the woods doing other things. There's certainly no rule that states you must feel less proud of a big buck you've killed just because you learned of his whereabouts while hunting for small game or cross-country skiing.

I'm sure most serious trophy whitetail hunters will agree that there's nothing quite as frustrating as having a mature buck seemingly dead to rights, only to have that deer somehow give us the slip. But no matter how good we get at this sport, there still are going to be more hunts when the final score rests in favor of our quarry. That's directly attributable to the caliber of the animals we're pursuing.

Still, I feel strongly that there are host of things we can do to help raise our personal success rates somewhat. Certainly, post-season scouting ranks near the very top of the list.

Greg's Proven Pointers

- The best in the sport will tell you that thoroughly scouting your hunting areas is vitally important—and this means scouting at all times of the year.

- Although certainly not a necessity, snow cover is a valuable asset. Having snow on the ground enables you to evaluate buck sign and determine how fresh that sign is.

- Post-season scouting starts by first pinpointing primary deer feeding areas. Then walk the outside perimeter of these feeding areas and check for buck sign.

- Your Number One priority during the post-season is to find the exact location of buck bedding areas. You can do this by following rub-lines away from feeding areas.

- Shed antlers can tell you a lot about the caliber of bucks in a specific area. But be forewarned: Finding sheds often entails spending a lot of hours and walking a lot of miles.

CHAPTER SEVEN

The Nocturnal Buck

Okay, so you've read the title of this chapter. If you've been involved in the sport of deer hunting for any length of time, I know it's a term you've heard many times. You also know exactly what it means—a whitetail buck that just refuses to play the game. Deer that fit into this category *never* leave the safety and security of their bedding areas during daylight hours—not for any reason! Of course, this makes them impossible to kill.

I guess one of the first things to do before proceeding is give you my definition for the term "nocturnal buck." I'm sure most hunters naturally assume I'm talking about bucks that don't move around at all during daylight hours. That's not quite true. You see, any buck that absolutely refuses to move around during legal shooting hours is virtually unkillable.

In this case, when I talk about nocturnal bucks, I'm referring to those deer that do the *majority* of their moving under the cover of darkness. What this means is that *some* of their traveling occurs during daylight hours—which, of course, makes them very killable.

Each year I have a good number of hunters tell me about big bucks they've chased throughout previous seasons. Quite a large percentage of these same hunters also tell me how they gave up on a certain big deer because he went totally nocturnal. "I kept finding fresh rubs and scrapes from a big buck I was chasing this past year," one frustrated hunter told me recently. "But even though I hunted him real hard, I never did get a look at that deer. I'm sure he was totally nocturnal." Maybe. Maybe not.

Any big buck that travels entirely after dark is virtually unkillable. On the other hand, if a big buck is moving around at all during daylight hours he is very killable—and certainly worth hunting!

I've had more than my share of encounters with nocturnal bucks over the many years I've been chasing whitetails. My first few experiences with these daylight-shy creatures left me with the same impression that I now see many modern day deer hunters harboring: Nocturnal bucks are impossible to kill!

But now I know for sure that this isn't always true. As I've learned, there are various forms of nocturnal buck behavior. More importantly, it's my belief that some hunters simply make the wrong interpretations from their observations. In other words, a big buck they suspect is nocturnal really isn't.

In this chapter I'm going to cover some of the key ingredients hunters need to effectively hunt nocturnal bucks. I'm also going to talk about why some hunters continually make the mistake of assuming that a particular big buck has gone underground (when in reality that deer is walking around quite a bit during daylight hours).

Focus on the Bedding Areas

The previous two chapters are a perfect lead-in for this chapter. That's because the most crucial ingredient necessary for successfully hunting nocturnal bucks is knowing the exact location of buck bedding areas. The best methods and times to accomplish this were covered in detail in Chapters Five and Six.

I remember well a trophy whitetail bowhunt I went on to Alberta, Canada, more than 10 years ago. The time was early fall, and the deer in our hunting area

The most important criteria for hunting a nocturnal buck is figuring out where that deer is bedding.

were in a strong feeding pattern. Initially, our morning and evening stands were placed fairly close to the main food source, which was an irrigated alfalfa field. It quickly became apparent, however, that this strategy wasn't going to work. The bucks simply weren't reaching our positions before dark in the afternoon. And they were well past us by the time daylight rolled around in the morning.

The logical solution was to move our stands farther back away from the field. But there was a problem. We could go just so far into the timber because there was only about 400 yards of available cover between the alfalfa field and a wide, deep river. The deer were bedding in a rather narrow, but thick, strip of thumb-sized willows that ran along the river's edge.

We tried placing our stands right on the edge of the willows, but the bucks were still going past us before legal shooting time in the morning. We also tried sitting on these stands in the afternoons. Unfortunately, each day dozens of antlerless deer would walk out of the bedding area some time before dark. Without fail, one of these deer would eventually get downwind of our stand positions. This deer would then make sure every antlered animal within hearing also knew we were there.

After thinking about it for a while, we finally came up with what we thought was a sure way to deal with the situation. We knew that, within an hour after dark, just about every deer living in the stretch of river-bottom would be feeding in the irrigated alfalfa. We figured this would be the best time to venture into the bedding area and put up a couple of stands—and that's exactly what we did.

To be safe, we left camp around 10 p.m., equipped with flashlights, treesteps and treestands. It took only a few minutes to walk back to the bedding area. Fortunately, we were able to find a couple of large cottonwood trees standing in the willows. A little over an hour later, our stands were in place. To ensure we'd be able to find our stands in the dark, we marked a walking trail with small reflective markers.

Long before daylight the next morning, and while all the deer were still in the alfalfa field, my hunting partner and I climbed up to the tree stands we'd placed the previous night. Thirty minutes before shooting time, I heard the first sounds of deer walking back into the bedding area. Ten minutes later I had deer all around me. I could hear them feeding, sparring and even bedding down. It was a terribly exciting time, believe me!

And when it finally got light enough to shoot? Well, unfortunately, the only antlered deer bedded within bow range of my stand site was a small 8-pointer. Interestingly, he was curled up and sound asleep...until I started climbing down from my stand! He immediately exploded out of his bed, which prompted several unseen and very large bucks to also jump and run. By the way, my partner also saw a small buck.

I still firmly believe that our game-plan for dealing with those nocturnal Alberta bucks was a sound one. After all, we had managed to get our stands in place right in the bedding area without disturbing the deer. And both my partner and I ended up with close range shots at bucks. The fact that we didn't end up having a big buck bed down right under our stands was just pure luck on the deers' part.

Nocturnal Bucks Require Creative Tactics

Several years ago, a hunter that lives near my hometown shot a tremendous buck during our state's archery season. I was talking to the guy about his successful hunt and asked him how he managed to take his trophy. His story had a very familiar ring to it.

"I'd seen the buck a number of times throughout the late summer and early fall," he said. "Every time I saw him, he was traveling with a couple of smaller bucks. I also noticed that the three bucks always came out of the same patch of woods. But there were problems. First, all three of the bucks went nocturnal right before bow season opened. And second, the woods where they were living was so small there was no way I could hunt there, even on the edge, without spooking the bucks."

The hunter spent the first few days of the archery season racking his brain in an attempt to figure out how he could get his stand placed in the woods. "Finally, I decided to do something off the wall," he told me. "I waited until the middle of the day and then took some treesteps and my stand and walked right into the woods. Of course, I jumped the bucks and they immediately ran out the other side of the woods, which is exactly what I wanted."

The successful hunter told me he didn't want to spend a lot of time in the bedding area. "I took just enough time to figure out exactly where the big buck was

There are times when you may have to come up with your own "off-the-wall" tactic for dealing with a nocturnal buck.

laying. Then I went ahead and put my stand up in a large oak tree. I'd have a fifteen yard shot to the buck's bedding spot—provided he returned."

The guy waited three days before returning to hunt from his stand in the small woods. "Since there was no way I'd be able to get into my stand while the bucks were in the bedding area, I'd have to do it when they weren't there," he said. "I figured the best time to do this would be during the early morning hours, long before daylight. Then it would just be a matter of having the bucks return and bed down in the same spots as before. I also had to pray none of the bucks would smell or hear me before it got light enough to shoot."

Fortunately, everything went according to plan. "About twenty minutes before daylight, I heard the bucks walk into the bedding area," the guy related. "They milled around a little bit and then they all laid down. Slowly, it started to get light. Eventually, I saw one of the smaller bucks. He was bedded right below my tree."

More daylight penetrated the thick patch of woods and the excited bowhunter finally made out the form of the big buck. "He was bedded right where I had hoped," he told me. "I waited a few more minutes, until it was fully light. Then, before drawing my bow, I made sure the small buck that was bedded below me was looking elsewhere." To shorten the story a bit, the guy made a perfect double-lung hit on the big buck.

In many cases, the key to killing a strictly nocturnal buck means pinpointing exactly where that deer is bedding. And not only must you find the exact spot where's he's sleeping away the daylight hours, you must also find a stand site that puts you within range of that spot. Obviously, you don't have to be quite so picky if you're hunting with a firearm. It's a different story, however, if you're hunting with archery equipment.

The next big key is getting into your stand site without being detected. You must also take care not to leave any clue that you've invaded a buck's bedroom. Rubber boots, odorless clothing and taking shower with odorless soap just prior to your hunt are all prime prerequisites for bedding area success. (Personally, I also wear one of those charcoal/carbon Scent-Lok suits.)

One more thing. Taking a big buck while sitting on a stand right in his bedding area is strictly dependent upon *everything* going right the very first time. This is one of those strategies where you're going to get only one chance to kill a particular trophy deer. After that, he will have caught on to your game plan. And if you think he was nocturnal before…

Calling: Try it During Afternoon Hunts

Trying to take a stubbornly nocturnal buck on afternoon hunts can be slightly more difficult. You'll notice I said difficult, not impossible. It usually entails employing a tactic that you may have used it in the past, but probably not in a situation like this.

Let's face it, if a buck is in a strict nocturnal movement pattern, he obviously isn't going to come waltzing out of his bedding area on his own. And you can't go into his daytime hideout and expect to shoot him out of his bed either. Still,

A bit of timely calling from the right location might entice an otherwise daylight-shy buck out of his daytime hideout.

I've found there is a way to get some daylight shy bucks to leave their bedding sanctuaries. And the best way to do this is by using a bit of timely calling.

As I already pointed out in Chapter Three, there are a couple of keys to successful calling for big bucks. One of these keys is altering your calling routine with each and every sequence. Another key is calling from different locations. Thankfully, most big bucks usually have a number of different points from which they will enter/exit their bedding areas. In most cases, these entrance/exit points are clearly marked with a series of antler rubs.

While you might be able to call-in some big bucks from stand sites located a good distance from their bedding areas, I'm afraid you won't see such results when dealing with nocturnal bucks. Your success rate is going to be directly related to getting your stands placed on the doorstep to buck bedding areas.

I remember a big woods 10-pointer I rattled-in and arrowed some years back. My success on that particular hunt was because of the fact that, during a spring scouting trip, I had managed to find the exact location of the buck's bedding area. I had then gone ahead and prepared a stand site right on the edge of that bedding area. A very convincing rattling sequence during the final stages of the pre-rut coaxed the buck out of his swampy sanctuary and to within 25 yards of where I waited. This was the very first time I had sat the stand.

I should point out that rattling and/or grunting isn't the only way you might be able to entice a buck out of his bedding area. In recent years, the use of doe

Bagging the Low Light/Nocturnal Buck

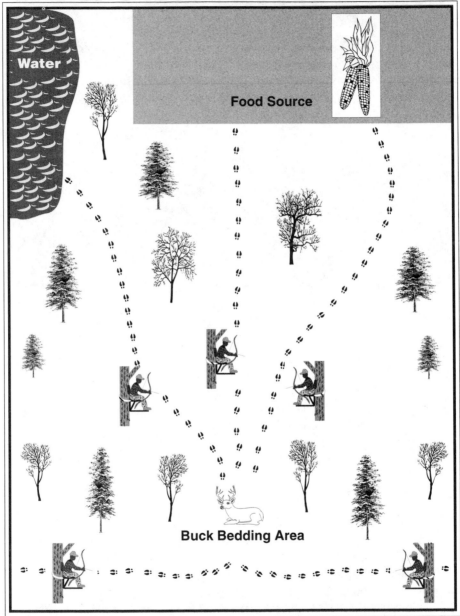

Water

Food Source

Buck Bedding Area

From what I've seen, there's only one truly effective way to deal with a low-light/nocturnal buck. You simply must set-up on the very edge of that deer's bedding area. You can either sit quietly and hope the deer walks by on his own or you can use a bit of calling to try and entice the buck out of his bedding area.

Stand Sites

**Buck Travel Routes
(Rub/Scrape-Lines)**

and fawn bleat calls has grown in popularity. I think bleat calls can be especially effective in those areas where the local buck population has been over-exposed to rattling antlers and grunt calls. Bleat calls also may invoke a high response rate in that three to five day period immediately preceding the actual rut.

But regardless of whether you choose to use rattling antlers, grunt calls, bleat calls or any combination thereof, your basic strategy for attempting to call-in a nocturnal buck should remain the same. To begin with, use the utmost care when approaching your stand sites. Take every precaution to avoid "bumping" other deer or alerting any other wildlife. Also, you simply can't make any unnatural noises, like the metal on metal sounds of treesteps clinking together, tree stand chains rattling, etc.

Before doing any calling, I like to wait until the movement and behavior of songbirds, squirrels, turkeys, etc. in the area around my stand site has returned to normal. Once I'm convinced the area has settled down, I'll then go through my one and only calling sequence for that particular stand sitting. That's right, anytime I know for certain I'm dealing with a very nocturnal buck, I call only once.

If there's one place where calling too often can be detrimental to your chances for success, this is that place! Look at it this way: If your stand is set up right on the edge of a buck bedding area, any big buck laying in that bedding area surely heard your first calling sequence. It's been my experience that if a buck is in the mood to check out some calling, he'll respond to your first effort—or not at all!

You should remember also that you're dealing with a buck that has already displayed very nocturnal tendencies. Contrary to what some hunters believe, any further calling attempts aren't going to make a deer like this more curious. Additional calling right near his bedding area will only make him highly suspicious—especially if that calling is coming from the exact same place each and every time.

I firmly believe that you should sit in at least a slightly different position each time you call. And I really think you increase your chances of having a big buck respond if your calling sequences are all a bit different. You might want to use only some mock rubbing one time, then only your grunt call the next time. Maybe you should try only bleat calls on your next hunt. Then the next time use a combination of some or all of your calls. Mix it up!

I believe that most big bucks are inclined to do a small bit of moving around during daylight—at least initially. But once these deer sense the slightest bit of human pressure, their demeanor instantly changes. Unfortunately, the first bit of human pressure they feel usually comes about because of some basic mistakes we as hunters are making. We are our own worst enemy in far too many cases!

Sometimes, You Just Have to Walk Away

I'd also like to address one other point regarding nocturnal bucks. I've long believed that there are a few whitetail bucks that are so concerned with survival, they just won't leave the safety and security offered by their impenetrable and perfectly located daytime hideouts. Nothing we can do—whether it's an attempt at strategic stand placement or even the most seductive calling efforts—will lure

Take care to keep your presence a secret from the deer you're hunting. Above all, don't get into the rut of spending all your hunting time occupying the same stand.

those deer out of hiding. We've even had trouble trying to run these deer out by sending several hunters through their bedding areas during gun-season.

In your pursuit of trophy whitetails there may come a time when you suspect a deer you're currently hunting fits this description. My advice is to simply walk away from that deer, regardless of how large he might be. Face it, you stand absolutely no chance of killing a buck that's totally nocturnal. Obviously then, your energies would be better spent hunting a buck that's a bit more cooperative.

Before ending this chapter, I want to touch on one last important point. There's always a possibility that a buck you suspect has gone into a strict nocturnal movement pattern really hasn't. This sort of thing happens more often than most hunters would believe. When it comes to figuring out exactly where a certain big buck is bedding, far too many hunters simply make educated guesses. And if my observations are accurate, a lot of these guesses are way off the mark.

Misinformation regarding the location of a big buck's bedding area often can lead a hunter to believe that a specific deer does all his traveling after dark. In truth, that deer might be quite daylight-active, but you're not aware of it simply because you're hunting all the wrong spots.

Singling out and then killing a mature whitetail buck—whether he's nocturnal or not—can prove to be a difficult chore. I can assure you it will be even more difficult if you have no idea where that deer is bedding.

Greg's Proven Pointers

- It's important to note that when a buck gets into a strict nocturnal movement pattern, he is virtually unkillable. You must learn how to recognize when you should display the good sense to walk away.

- The most effective way to deal with nocturnal/low-light active bucks is to set-up on the doorstep to their bedding areas.

- Calling can be a great way to entice a daylight-shy buck out of his bedding area during legal shooting time. However, I strongly recommend you keep your calling efforts to a minimum!

- Often, bucks that are suspected of being nocturnal really aren't. In most cases this happens because of misinformation regarding the location of the deer's bedding areas.

CHAPTER EIGHT

The Solo Approach

Before you continue reading any further, I'd like to make a few important statements about this chapter. First and foremost, I don't consider this chapter to be required reading for every deer hunter. Secondly, I'm not in any way inferring that, to be successful at taking mature bucks, you must apply a solo approach to *every* aspect of your hunting endeavors. Lastly, you should know that the information contained herein definitely is aimed more at bow-hunters than gun hunters.

While I'm on the subject of bow-hunting, allow me to state an undeniable fact. To consistently make accurate, killing shots, even the most proficient bow-hunters need to have their quarry literally in their laps. It's also a fact that there's no way you'll be able to accomplish this feat unless the animals you're hunting are totally unaware of your presence. If I've learned one thing during the 30-plus years I've been bow-hunting, it's that trying to keep our presence a secret from the animals we're hunting is an extremely difficult task.

I believe many hunters are under the impression that remaining hidden from the mature bucks in their hunting areas is their one and only worry. But this just isn't the case. More times than not, big buck success is going to hinge directly on keeping your presence a secret from all the deer in your hunting areas.

The importance of keeping a low profile was made obvious to me years ago on some of my first bow-hunts. I quickly learned that if the first deer that passed by my stand site (whether it was a small buck, doe or fawn) blew the whistle on my location, my hunt for that day usually was ruined. In most cases, I'd see no further activity by the whitetail herd in that area for the remainder of my hunting time.

Here's the bottom line—getting a trophy-sized whitetail buck within bow range can be an extremely difficult task *even when you're hunting alone.* So let

Slipping into and out of your hunting areas without creating a distrubance is a big key to big buck success. This can be difficult for one person to pull off; it's nearly impossible when two people are invading the same area.

me ask you this question: How on earth do you expect to score on a monster buck if you insist on dragging a buddy (or two or three) with you every time you venture into the heart of your favorite big buck hot spots?

Even if you and your hunting partners are extremely careful about every aspect of bow-hunting for trophy whitetail deer, I still feel strongly that the solo approach is best. Remember, twice as many people means twice as much human odor, twice as much noise and twice as much general disturbance in a particular area. And if you think for one second that such disturbances aren't going to be detected by a mature buck, think again!

Changing Quarry Means Changing Attitudes

Those bow-hunters who are just making the transition from mere "deer hunter" to "trophy hunter" must be aware of something else. Although you might have been able to get away with certain things when hunting immature bucks, this will end the very second you limit your efforts exclusively to older age-class animals.

Again, all this points to one very obvious fact. If you're truly serious about killing larger, more mature bucks, you might have to change your approach to the sport. This means that "gang-hunting" definitely is out of the question. In fact, if you're serious about killing mature bucks, I'd strongly suggest reducing the number of hunters in your group down to one. In other words, go solo!

Why am I so adamant about adopting a solo approach? Well, let's say you and a prospective hunting partner are doing some in-season scouting. After a bit of looking around, you happen to find the stomping grounds of what you know has to be a great buck. The deer is rubbing on trees the size of your lower leg—and you find a lot of these large rubs! Also, there are scrapes everywhere. With the way the scrapes have been worked, you just know the buck is freshening his odorous signposts on a regular basis.

As luck would have it, you find a tree that lies well within bow range of the trail the buck appears to be using most often. In a matter of minutes, the tree is prepared and readied for your portable stand. Later, you meet up with your partner back at the vehicle and immediately tell him about your findings. Funny, he doesn't seem all that excited. Hmmmmm...

Because this is such an impressive animal, you adopt a very disciplined hunting regimen. You hunt from the stand no more than three times a week, and then only if the wind direction is absolutely perfect. But even with this very cautious approach, it appears the buck hasn't worked any of his scrapes in recent days. You also notice that no fresh rubs have appeared lately. It's almost like that one trip into his core area was enough to scare off the record book animal.

But then you have a long talk with your new hunting partner. After a bit of insistent questioning about his actions on the scouting day, he finally comes clean. Your "buddy" admits that, while you were busy preparing the tree, he had given in to an irresistible call of nature. Unbelievably, the guy "relaxed his bowels" only 75 yards from your stand site. And because he had no toilet paper with him, he had no choice but to cut-up his underwear and use that. Of course, the underwear is still laying out in the woods—75 yards from your stand!

This illustrates prefectly the point I'm trying to make. You have complete control over all of your actions while you're out in the woods. But you really have no control over what your hunting partner(s) might do, especially once they are out of your sight. Even though you might be extremely careful about things like human odor, unnatural noises or going to the bathroom in the heart of a big buck's core area, your efforts might well be for naught.

Maybe one of your hunting partner tells you that his hunting clothes have been washed in odorless detergent. But is that truly the case? Also, has he been as careful as you about his personal hygiene? More importantly, what's this person doing when he's sitting on his stand? Is he *really* being as careful as he claims regarding keeping a low profile while hunting?

As you might imagine, I've had more than my share of hunting buddy experiences over the years. But an incident that happened a few years back comes to mind most readily.

I had spent the better part of our bow season hunting with one particular individual. Now, we weren't actually hunting together per-se, rather I was hunting one area and he was hunting another. However, we were staying in the same camp and riding back and forth from our hunting areas in the same vehicle.

As it sometimes goes in bow-hunting, I was seeing deer on every outing. It wasn't the same for my friend, however. After nearly a month's worth of hunts,

Remember, once he is out of your sight, you have no control over what a "buddy" does. You have to wonder, is he being as careful as he claims?

he had yet to see his first deer. Being somewhat concerned about this, and not wanting to appear selfish, I decided to take the guy into one of my better spots. My plan was to have him place his stand in a tree approximately 100 yards from my stand site. Beforehand, however, I made sure he understood all the requirements regarding noise, human odor, etc. My partner assured me he would play by my rules.

On the first afternoon we hunted together, and for the first time all season, I failed to see a single deer. Later, I learned that my partner hadn't seen anything either. For lack of a better excuse, I passed it off merely to bad luck. However, this same deerless trend continued for the next few outings. Eventually, my friend became disgusted and decided to move on to another area. I agreed to take down his tree stand and bring it out with me on the next trip I made into the area.

It wasn't until I climbed the tree to take down my partner's stand that I got the complete story of why this area had suddenly gone cold There, laying on the platform of his stand, were the extinguished butts from at least a half-dozen cigarettes. After a bit of looking, I found several more laying on the ground directly under his stand. Obviously, my friend had spent the duration of his time on stand puffing away. It doesn't take a genius to figure out what sort of an effect the odor had on the deer herd in that area.

This reinforces the statement I made earlier. You might have complete control over the actions of your hunting partners *while you can see them.* However,

I spend a lot of time hunting with my brother, Jeff. But Jeff and I never trespass into each other's designated hunting spots during the open season.

that control ceases the minute they are out of your sight. At that point, they become free to do whatever they please. And if they truly are acting irresponsibly, the result is often a rapid deterioration in the quality of some of your best hunting spots.

Hunting Solo—With a Partner

Anyone who has read some of the many magazine articles I've written knows that I spend a lot of time chasing big whitetail bucks with my brother Jeff. Yes, Jeff and I spend a lot of time together during the open season. However, none of this time is spent *hunting together*. Let me explain.

The first thing Jeff and I do whenever we gain access to a new tract of hunting land is to scout the area thoroughly. The we split the area as equally as possible. This equal split doesn't necessarily mean we each get 50 percent of the property either. Rather, Jeff and I try to split the quality hunting spots equally. Of course, this means there have been occasions when we've established stand sites relatively close to each other. However, we make it a point to *never* hunt from those stands on the same days.

Even though I know that Jeff is just as careful and meticulous as me in his pre-hunt preparations, I still don't want him hunting too close to me. And he feels exactly the same way. This isn't selfishness, either. It's merely a matter of having gained some real insight into the way mature whitetails react to even the smallest amount of human intrusion. Again, it's hard enough for one person to go into and out of an area without causing some kind of disturbance. With two people, there's twice as much chance of having something go wrong.

Jeff and I often ride together to our hunting areas. But when we step out of the vehicle, he goes his way and I go mine. The next time we see each other is when we meet back at the vehicle after the hunt is over. Then we take a few minutes to compare notes on the events that took place on that particular hunt. We often continue to talk about our hunt and possibly discuss some different strategies on the drive home.

This brings up another important point. Going solo for big bucks doesn't necessarily mean you have to isolate yourself from people for the duration of the open season. It merely means that anytime you venture into one of your prime hunting spots, you should do so alone. The time to get together with friends and hunting partners is back at your vehicle, at home or in camp. In fact, I encourage you to do this very thing. And for a very specific reason.

A good hunting partner can prove to be a very valuable asset during those "down times" so common to bow-hunters. Nothing is more comforting or reassuring after an extremely close-call, missed shot or blown opportunity, like a few well-chosen words from the right person. Personally, I've been blessed to have known more than my share of people who possessed the ability to always say the right things at the right times.

Along with Jeff, there are several other individuals with whom I spend some time during the open archery season. But just like with my brother, we actually spend very little of this time together in the woods. And unless we are trailing a wounded deer or providing assistance in getting a downed animal out of the woods, we make it a point to *always* stay away from each other's hunting areas.

The Value of Friends—Before and After a Hunt

My good friend and hunting partner Tom Indrebo and I have a sort of tradition we follow. Before heading out to our individual hunting areas in the morning, we sit around the breakfast table and discuss our plan of attack over a couple cups of coffee. In most cases, we then meet back at camp during the midday hours to compare notes on the morning hunt and also to see if anybody in our group needs assistance. We also use this time to grab a bite to eat and go over our strategies for the afternoon hunt. Once the afternoon hunt is completed, we meet back at camp. It's time once again to share our experiences and see if someone needs help trailing or getting a buck out of the woods.

Actually, this sort of interaction has led me to become very close with several individuals. And this closeness has come about even though *we never have actually hunted together!*

My buddies and I have learned the hard way just how hypersensitive and naturally reclusive mature bucks can be. Hence, we know that the most effective

Mature bucks are hypersensitive and naturally reclusive creatures. The most effective way to deal with these traits is to adopt a solo approach.

way to hunt these animals is through a solo approach. I'm sure most serious trophy whitetail hunters will attest that this is the exact approach needed to realize regular success on big bucks.

I'd like to point out that your solo efforts need not carry over into non-hunting times. Exploring new areas, off-season scouting and searching for shed antlers are all examples of endeavors that hunting partners can do together. Also, stand-site selection and preparation is a chore that often times begs for assistance from a partner. Again, provided this is done during the off-season, there is no harm in having someone accompany you into your hunting areas.

But there's another very important reason for taking someone along when selecting and preparing stand sites. Anytime you head into the woods, for any reason, someone should be aware of exactly where you'll be. These people should also have some idea of what time you'll be coming out of the woods. Why? Well, if you fail to show up at the designated time, they can instigate what might very well prove to be a life-saving search. And because they know exactly where you're hunting, your partners won't waste precious time looking in all the wrong places.

Don't think for a second that bad things only happen to other bow-hunters either. Nowadays, the majority of people who bow-hunt for whitetails spend most of their hunting time perched in tree stands. This means it's entirely possible that *anyone* could suffer a serious injury at any time.

As far too many hunters have found out, a crippling injury can happen in the blink of an eye. Sometimes these accidents occur even though we've taken every conceivable precaution. You must admit, if you're laying on the ground unable to move, it would be quite comforting to know that it's just a matter of time before you'll get some much needed assistance.

It's important to remember that the approach I've discussed in this chapter is most important to those aspiring to become consistently successful on trophy class whitetail bucks. If what I've seen and heard in recent years is any indication, the majority of those who bow-hunt for whitetail deer have a burning desire to increase their success rate on trophy size animals. So I guess it's safe to assume that the solo approach is right for a lot of people.

Loners—Or Just Smart Hunters?

Interestingly, the majority of highly successful trophy whitetail hunters I know are pretty much "loners." Of course, I've heard other not-quite-so-successful hunters make comments as to why they think these people spend so much of the season hunting alone. "They don't want anybody tagging along with 'em because they're shooting all their deer after dark," one disgruntled hunter told me. "How else could they be killing so many big bucks?"

Yes, most successful big buck hunters are loners. But it isn't because they're doing illegal things. They've adopted a solo approach because they've discovered one of the biggest keys to success in this sport. You must keep the animals you're hunting from ever realizing they're being hunted. And the one sure way to consistently pull this off is by hunting alone. This is the real reason why "loners" kill so many big deer!

I've talked extensively about how important a solo approach is for taking mature bucks. But what aspiring trophy hunters must realize is that there actually are different classes of mature whitetails. The same strategies that work to consistently get you within range of three-year-old bucks won't necessarily work to get you shots at four- and five-year-old animals.

Some of you reading this may be ready to make the jump to that next level of trophy whitetail hunting. You've already taken a fair number of 130 to 140-class bucks. You're now looking to shoot some 150-class animals. Well folks, if you

Going solo does not mean you must totally isolate yourself from other hunters during the season. In fact, there are times you may need the assistance of several buddies.

think it was tough getting three-year-old bucks to walk by within bow range, just wait until you raise your standards to the next level. No doubt about it. The solo approach is an absolute mandatory requirement now.

There are some who may look upon this chapter as being a slam against establishing friendships in the sport of bow-hunting. I totally disagree. In fact, I believe I've clearly pointed out that it's entirely possible to establish friendships *and* find some top-notch hunting partners even while maintaining a solo approach.

Others may regard the 'going solo' technique as being somewhat radical and unnecessary. I'll admit, that may be the case for some deer hunters. Not everyone who is involved in the sport of deer hunting has visions of upping their success rate on mature bucks. Perhaps their current hunting style is extremely effective on immature bucks and antlerless deer, which is all that matters to them.

As I'm writing this, I've just taken on a most special hunting partner. My son Jake is now old enough to join me in the woods. For most of my son's first couple of years of hunting, my portable stand will be placed in the same tree as his. And those times when I'm not sitting right alongside him, I'll still be within sight.

I realize that such an arrangement might be detrimental to Jake's chances for success on a real whopper buck. However, my main concern at this point is to allow him plenty of time to become comfortable with this whole hunting deal.

Also, Jake's personal goal his first season is to shoot a buck with six-points or better. This means we will primarily be hunting immature animals.

Still, I know the day is coming when my son will want to raise his standards and try for a mature buck. At that point, he will surely want to "go solo." Because I know this is such a crucial ingredient in trophy whitetail hunting, I'll gladly honor Jake's wish and step aside.

Greg's Proven Pointers

- The most important prerequisite for consistently getting big bucks within bow range is keeping your presence a secret from those deer.

- Although a hunting partner might claim to be careful, you have no idea if this is true, and you have no control over what that individual does once he's out of your sight.

- It's okay to have a hunting partner(s). However, I strongly urge that you never "trespass" into each other's chosen hunting spots.

- While I believe that a solo approach is critical for big buck success, you shouldn't take it to extremes. For safety reasons, make sure that someone always knows where you'll be hunting.

CHAPTER NINE

Solving the Time Puzzle

Several years ago I received a letter from a fellow Midwestern deer hunter, who wrote that he had discovered the whereabouts of a huge whitetail buck. He added that through careful scouting he been able to pinpoint the location of the buck's core area. The man had then placed several portable tree stands to take advantage of the patterns he had unraveled.

I thought the letter wasn't unlike many I receive each year, until I read the last paragraph. If I remember right, the exact wording went something like, "I've learned a lot about the big buck over the past several weeks. I know where he likes to feed, where his favorite travel routes are located and also where he beds during the day. I don't want to waste a lot of time on my stands, so my question to you is this. Can you tell me what time I can expect the buck to move?"

I'm sure everyone reading this has heard the old saying, "timing is everything." I'd be willing to bet that most hunters are fully aware of just how pertinent that saying is to the sport of deer hunting. A few minutes here or there often spells the difference between failure or success.

I'd also be willing to bet that most deer hunters have, at some point, wished they could come up with some way to accurately predict exactly when a big buck was going to walk by their stands. After all, this would eliminate much of the guesswork associated with hunting for trophy whitetails. From that point forward, our success rates would go nowhere but up!

I'm sure the majority of deer hunters have thought about how nice it would be if they could figure out exactly when to be on their stands.

Patience—One of Our Strongest Weapons

Successful trophy whitetail hunting is, more than anything else, a waiting game. I believe patience might be as important as any of the other weapons in our arsenal. After all, the greatest trophy hunting strategies are of no benefit if we don't have the patience to allow those strategies to work.

I must admit, there was once a time when patience wasn't one of my stronger attributes. In fact, it was a rare occasion when I managed to sit in one place for more than an hour. As you might imagine, my ants-in-the-pants approach resulted in far more unsuccessful than successful seasons.

I remember an experience I had many years ago on the opening day of my home state's gun-season for deer. After spending a mere hour on my stand, I decided to leave the woods and head back to my cabin to get some breakfast. Two hours later, and with a full belly, I headed back out to my stand.

Upon arriving back at my stand site, a very disheartening sight met my unbelieving stare. Everywhere I looked, fresh, running deer tracks crisscrossed the snow. What was most interesting is that there had been only a couple of deer tracks within sight of my stand when I'd left two hours earlier.

It didn't take a genius to figure out what had transpired. From the looks of things, a "hot" doe had lead a big buck on a merry chase all around my stand site. What a show that would have been, to say nothing of the opportunity I'd have had to kill that buck. If only I had stayed on my stand for an hour longer!

Thankfully, I've been able to overcome my impatience. And it has paid big dividends. Take, for instance, a big buck I shot several years ago. Initially, it was my intent on the fateful day to stay on my stand until 9:30 a.m.. At that time, I was going to relocate to a stand in another part of the woods where I was hunting. My 9:30 deadline came and went, however. Since I was quite comfortable, I decided to stay put for a while longer. The next time I looked at my watch, it was 10:15.

Fifteen minutes later, I heard what I thought were the sounds of a man walking down the open oak ridge behind me. I turned my head, fully expecting to see a hunter heading my way. But that's not quite what I saw. Instead, a dandy 10-point buck was walking directly at me. With his head held high, the buck was taking long, ground-covering strides. I remember thinking that this was going to be almost too easy. As it was, I ended up shooting the buck at a range of 15 yards.

Granted, the decision to stay on my stand had been made on the spur of the moment. Yet it had paid off in a big way. Had I stuck to my original plan, I would have been long gone when the buck walked by my stand.

Nothing will ensure that you'll be in the woods at the right time like extending the time you spend in the woods. Let me add something else. If you're reading this chapter in the hopes of discovering some secret formula for figuring out *exactly* when you should be on your stands, you might as well quit reading and move on to the next chapter. No matter what you might have read or heard, *there's no way of accurately predicting exactly when a mature buck is going to move.*

Over the years I've had a number of hunters tell me they felt certain a big buck was walking past one of their stand sites. Trouble is, they didn't know exactly what time the buck was doing this. Even though his rubs and scrapes were freshened routinely, he never did come ambling by when they were waiting on their stand.

Of course, I usually tell these individuals there's always the possibility the buck is moving strictly under the cover of darkness. But a lot of hunters tell me they don't believe this is the case. In fact, some of these guys have told they jumped big bucks while walking into their hunting spot. (Which only added to their frustration.) The eventual and obvious question I then get asked is, "Can you tell me how I can figure out what time I should be on my stand?"

Breaking Old Habits

Just like the deer we hunt, humans are creatures of habit. Often, we follow the same routine every time we go into a certain area. Not only do we walk into and out of our stand sites at the same time, we use the exact same routes. Could it be that the bucks in your hunting areas know exactly when it's safe to move around because they've got you timed? I believe this is the case more times than not, especially if the target of your desires happens to be a mature animal.

Although exact timing is important, I still believe that a hunter's greatest ally is patience.

Hunters are notorious for walking into and out of their hunting areas at the same times every day. This is a big reason deer, even fawns, are able to pattern hunters so easily.

There are some simple solutions for keeping the bucks we're hunting from timing our actions. For instance, one effective strategy is to stagger the times you walk into your hunting area. Another thing you can do is to figure out a couple of different approach routes to your stands. Alternate using these different routes each time you walk into the stand site.

Without a doubt, the main reason whitetails are able to accurately time so many hunters is because those hunters are guilty of overhunting a certain spot. No matter how often they've sat on the stand in the past, and regardless of which direction the wind is blowing, they sit on this same stand every time they hunt.

I can't stress enough how detrimental such an approach is to your chances for success. Remember, one of the big keys to success in this sport is to keep the deer guessing. Not only do we want them guessing about *where* we might be, we also want them guessing about *when* we're going to be there. And the only way to do this is by constantly rotating our stand sittings. From what I've seen, this is the best way to throw off a big buck's timing.

If you think about it, this is exactly why mature whitetails are such tough customers. They constantly keep *us* guessing, not only as to where they might show up, but also when they're going to be there. And very seldom do they show up in the exact same place at the exact same time two days in a row. They constantly rotate their travel routes.

Some hunters use timing devices in an attempt to figure out the "right time" to be in the woods. I have to admit, I've used these handy little gadgets and found them to extremely accurate and reliable. The rap I have against them is that you're still left out in the dark when it comes to distinguishing the sex or size of the deer tripping the timer. As many hunters have discovered, you can end up wasting valuable time hunting a deer that, when it finally does walk into view, falls far short of your expectations.

In recent years I've done a bit of experimenting with those timing/camera devices. The obvious advantage of these things is that they not only tell you what time an animal walked through a certain spot, they also provide you with a photo of that animal. Surely, this can go a long way toward answering the infamous "what time is the right time" question. Right?

Not really. If I've learned one thing from fooling around with the timer/camera gadgets, it's that mature whitetail bucks are even more unpredictable than I originally believed. Even though they might visit the same spot on several occasions, *none* of the mature bucks we've photographed did so at the same times twice in a row. And they weren't off by just a few minutes either—it was more like hours.

Another thing. We've found absolutely no evidence that moon phases had any bearing on when a big deer would move. Nor were we able to predict, again by studying moon phases, where a buck would show up. But more on the "lunar thing" a bit later.

Improve Odds by Increasing Hunting Time

So what's the answer to the age-old question of "When is the best time to be on my stand?" The obvious answer is to be there at the exact time when the buck you want walks by. Trying to figure out when that event occurs may be the most difficult task facing trophy whitetail hunters.

Part of the problem lies in the fact that there still are far too many deer hunters who think that early morning and late afternoon are the only times worth hunting. I'll admit these have proven to be prime deer movement times. However, when we figure in such huge variables as the rut and hunting pressure, all the rules governing early morning/late afternoon hunting can be thrown out the window.

I'm not going to blow a lot of smoke and pretend I know exactly when I should be on my stands. I spend a lot of time in the woods. I think you'll find this also to be the case with trophy whitetail hunters who happen to be a lot more successful than me. In talking to some of these fellows you realize just how much time they spend hunting every year. Once more, you can't shoot 'em if you aren't out there!

As I stated previously, I believe that the more time we spend hunting, the more we increase our chances of being successful. This rule applies to everyone and at all times. For instance, if you've got a half-hour of free time before you have to go to work or school, why not spend that half-hour on your stand?

Now, I'll agree, it might seem ridiculous to go through all the preparation you normally do for an all-day hunt, just to spend a mere 15 or 30 minutes on a stand. But remember, the right time can be any given moment of any given day.

Big bucks normally are low-light/nocturnal movers. However, things like hunting pressure and the different phases of the rut can have huge bearing on when bucks move.

This might be hard to believe, but during our bow season a few years ago, I shot a buck and had him dead on the ground after spending less than one minute in my tree-stand. That buck was definitely proof that timing is everything. It's also concrete evidence that *anytime can be the right time!*

I have a habit of looking at my watch to check the time as soon as a deer walks into sight. On this particular day, I had climbed to my stand and was pulling my bow up when I heard a twig snap. Looking in the direction of the sound, I saw a whitetail buck coming directly at me. The time was 2:23 p.m.

It took the buck just a few seconds to walk into bow range. In fact, I barely had time to unsnap the tow-rope from my bow, nock an arrow, pick an opening, draw and shoot. The hit was a perfect double lung job.

Instead of running off, however, the buck jumped straight into the air, took two steps and stood looking around. Then he tipped over dead just eight yards away. The time on my digital watch still read 2:23 p.m.! See what I mean about timing?

More than just a few of the best deer hunters I know have admitted to me that they believe in the power of a sixth sense. I know for a fact it has played a big role in my own success. The above related incident is just one example.

Normally, at the time of year when I shot the buck, I wouldn't have gone to my stand until almost three o'clock. But for some reason, I had an overwhelming urge to get on my stand a little earlier than usual on that day. Because of past experiences, I've learned to trust my urges or hunches or whatever you want to call them. Doing so has paid off just too many times.

Making Your Time Investment Pay Off

I once hunted with a guy who shared equally in my enthusiasm for hunting big woods whitetails. Like me, this fellow knew that sign interpretation was the one tried-and-true way of finding hunting hot spots in such an environment. It wasn't hard to convince him of the value of off-season scouting.

Anyway, the two of us spent a lot of time one spring searching for a big buck to hunt during the next bow season. Together, he and I finally found the sign of what we knew had to be a real whopper. This deer consistently rubbed on poplar trees as big around as my upper leg.

My friend and I went to work trying to decipher the travel pattern of the buck. Eventually, we were able to find the buck's main travel route and exactly where he was bedding. We went ahead and prepared a stand site that would allow my buddy to take advantage of this information. Both of us knew it was now just a matter of waiting until prime time next season.

My partner hunted the big buck once during the third week of October, but saw nothing. A week later, I called the guy to see if he was going to accompany me to my cabin and hunt the big buck again. "I can't make it," he informed me. "Something unexpected has come up. Sorry." I was sorry too. The monster bucks of the big woods were in the final stages of their pre-rut rituals. This was the best time to catch one of these normally reclusive animals moving along their established routes during legal shooting hours.

Anyway, my brother Jeff had tagged a buck earlier in the season, so he volunteered to make the trip with me. The first morning of my hunt, Jeff informed me of his plans. "I'll drop you off at your hunting area, then I'm going to drive around and see if I can spot any big bucks."

Jeff checked several known crossing points and then decided to drive through the area where my buddy was supposed to be hunting. Guess what was standing right in the middle of the road when my brother got there? You know it—the buck we'd scouted. He was late in getting back to his bedding area that morning. Everything we had suspected about the deer was confirmed. My brother said the buck's body and antler size were both of massive proportions.

What's most interesting is that the buck was traveling along the rub-line my buddy had been hunting. Further, all conditions were right for him to hunt from the stand on the day Jeff saw the buck. So he no doubt would have been waiting when the big buck walked by. Unfortunately, unforeseen circumstances had made it impossible for him to make the trip—bad timing.

This brings up a very important point about the time factor. All the scouting in the world will be to no avail if you don't apply what you've learned toward being on your stand at the right time. Look at it this way, if you spend 25, 50 or 100 hours scouting a certain big buck, doesn't it seem practical that you should spend at least a few hours hunting him—especially during prime-time? Again, it's impossible to kill any big buck if you're not out there trying.

This is my basic philosophy: If you spend many hours scouting a certain big buck during the off-season, then it only stands to reason you should spend at least a few days hunting that animal—especially during prime-time!

Timing Is Everything

There are many other instances I could relate concerning the right time, but one in particular comes to mind. This tale involves a fellow bow-hunter I met a few years ago. Unfortunately, his story doesn't have a happy ending either, but it does prove my point about timing being everything.

This hunter was walking into his stand site one early November afternoon when he saw a grouse. The bird offered a tempting target, so my acquaintance pulled an arrow out of his quiver and took a shot. He missed the bird and then spent some time looking for the errant shaft. Eventually he found it and then continued on toward his stand site.

Upon arriving at his destination, the bow-hunter tied one end of his tow rope onto his bow and put the other end in his teeth. Then he started climbing up to his tree-stand. When he was on the third step, he heard some brush breaking behind him. Turning and looking in the direction of the noise, he got the surprise of his life.

Less than 20 yards away stood a huge buck. The rutting deer had his head down, sniffing the ground. Then he started walking right toward the surprised hunter. The guy relating the story to me said he had never experienced such a feeling of helplessness. "I didn't dare move," he explained, "so I just stood there on that tree-step with my tow rope hanging out of my mouth and watched that buck walk right under me. He nearly stepped on my bow!

"When the deer got out to a range of about 25 yards, I hurriedly climbed the rest of the way to my stand and quickly pulled my bow up. But by the time I got the tow rope untied, the buck was out of range." The fellow then added, "If I hadn't stopped to fool with that partridge I would have been in my stand and ready when the eight pointer came by." Of course, he had no idea the time he spent fooling with the bird was going to cost him a chance at a buck—more bad timing.

Earlier, I mentioned that when hunting whitetails, I'm prodded to do something because of an overpowering urge or feeling I get. Many other successful deer hunters have told me they also get these feelings. On occasion these hunches, urges or feelings will prove to be a priceless aid in trying to establish the exact time you should be on your stand or in the woods. Although not every single hunch has meant a dead buck, enough of them have that I believe we'd be wise to pay attention to them. (There will be more on this in a later chapter.)

Some hunting and fishing magazines have charts that supposedly show the peak times to be on the water or in the woods. One of these charts says something to the effect that "the peaks indicated reflect the exact time of maximum game movement." Hmmmm…interesting, to say the least.

But perhaps nothing has caused more stir in the sport of deer hunting in recent years than the new "lunar" game movement guides. Supposedly, these lunar guides can not only tell you what time the deer are going to move, they can also tell you exactly where your stand should be placed.

Some people may tell you that these things are absolutely fool-proof. However, I tend to shy away from any gimmick that supposedly allows you to predict peak deer movement times. Why? Simply because it's just too much of a cut and dried thing to say that the deer are absolutely going to be moving at an exact time on a certain day and in a specific place.

The most important thing prospective trophy hunters must remember is that big bucks don't play by any set of rules. In my opinion, most whitetail timing guides are exactly that—a set of rules the deer are *supposed* to follow. *Nothing* will get you in more trouble and lead to more unsuccessful hunts than expecting a mature whitetail buck to abide by a set of human rules.

I'd like to end this chapter by sharing something with you. The enthusiasm and sheer love I still feel for this sport after 33 seasons is generated by one simple fact: Nothing else I've ever done in my lifetime has proved quite as challenging. A great part of this challenge exists because *there's still no way to accurately predict exactly what time a mature whitetail buck is going to move.*

If the day ever does come when we're able to accurately predict exactly what time a big buck is going to move and exactly where he's going to walk, every bit of the challenge will be gone from this sport. At that time, I'll be the first to hang up my bows and guns.

And that, my fellow hunters, comes straight from the heart!

Greg's Proven Pointers

- There's only one thing I'd like to point out in this chapter: Regardless of what you might have heard or read, there is NO WAY to time the appearance of mature bucks in specific spots. When it comes to "timing deer," patience always has been and remains our best ally.

CHAPTER TEN

The Grass Isn't Always Greener

I saw it just about every day at my construction job. A worker would be given an assigned task. Most times, the guy would complete the task in a prompt and satisfactory manner. However, all the while he was working, he was eyeing one of his fellow workers and grumbling about how "that guy over there has a lot easier job than me."

Ironically, in nearly every case where I saw this happen, the worker who was doing the grumbling eventually got his turn to do that "easier job." Almost without fail, the guy would work only a few minutes before he'd start grumbling about how much he disliked his new job. In fact, he wished he was back doing his other job. It seems the grass wasn't quite as green on this side of the fence as he originally thought.

In recent years, I've seen countless examples of this same mentality in the sport of deer hunting. Heck, I've been a victim myself of the "grass is greener on the other side of the fence" syndrome—and more than just a couple of times. I should add, however, that I've learned how to fight off the temptation this feeling creates. The result has been a rise in my big buck success rate.

It's my opinion that quite a few deer hunters are under the impression that the hunting, and certainly the quality of the bucks, is always better somewhere else. What I find amazing is that the vast majority of people who have expressed this opinion to me have never hunted more than 50 miles from home. Somehow, their minds conjure up visions of big buck havens that exist in remote areas. Of course, these "remote" areas are always just out of their reach.

But it really makes no difference if this big buck hot spot is in the next state, in a Canadian province or only 100 miles away. These guys will probably never take the time or spend the money and effort it takes to substantiate their suspicions. Therefore, they feel safe in making assumptions about the place.

Far too many hunters are under the false impression that the quality of the hunting and the caliber of the bucks is always better somewhere else.

What is it that leads hunters to believe that their chances for killing a big buck are better some place other than where they're currently hunting? Basically, I believe it's due in great part to our basic human emotions. If we feel we're doing everything within our power to kill a big deer, yet we still haven't connected, then we're obviously hunting a tough area. Or it could be that there just aren't any big bucks in the areas we're hunting.

These two assumptions might prove true in some cases. However, I believe there are just as many instances when they aren't. But whether they're true or not, making such statements somehow has a way of soothing our egos. Let's face it, not many self-professed trophy hunters want to admit that a flaw in their hunting tactics may be the reason that big bucks are able to constantly evade them.

Hidden Resources Right Under Your Nose

I saw a perfect example of the grass-is-always-greener mentality some years back when a friend and I were competing in two-man bass-fishing tournaments. My buddy and I fished a number of these events over a three-year period. We never took first place in any of the contests, but it seemed we were always able to put enough fish in the boat to at least win back our entry fee.

What's interesting about this is that I don't really think we were necessarily better fisherman than the guys we were beating. It was more a matter of paying attention to the way things went during each tournament and then acting accordingly.

Although my bass boat had a motor large enough to really get up and go, I was lacking sufficient horsepower to keep up with the real big boys. Usually, by the time we reached a spot we knew was holding fish, someone would already be working the area. Because of this, my partner and I realized we had to come up with a different strategy.

One thing became apparent right away. It seemed that all the other fisherman were in a big hurry to get as far away from the starting point as possible. When the signal to "GO" was given to each flight, the big outboards would roar to life and the streamlined bass boats would jump up out of the water and go streaking off toward distant destinations.

What my partner and I quickly learned is that none of the fisherman paid much attention to the water right near the launch area—which is exactly where my partner and I started concentrating our efforts. Usually, I wouldn't even crank up my big motor. I'd just kick the trolling motor into gear and we'd start working the shoreline right at the take-off point. Like I said, we did well enough to bring in money almost every time we entered a tournament.

I've discovered that deer hunters are a lot like those guys I fished with years ago. Instead of hunting close to home, they're inclined to jump in their vehicles and roar off to some distant destination. And if they hunt close to home, they don't give it their all. Why? Usually, it's because they're convinced there aren't any big bucks in the area.

Because we spend the majority of our time close to home, it just stands to reason that if a big buck is living somewhere close by, we'd have seen or heard about that deer, right? Not necessarily. In fact, I think that a lot of hunters would find it hard to believe that there might be a big buck residing just down the road from their homes.

This is directly attributable to a fact I've stressed repeatedly in this book: Mature whitetails are special creatures, no matter where they're found. If they don't want you to see them, you're not going to see them. I hasten to add that this is just as true of mature bucks found in highly populated areas as it is of mature bucks that reside in wilderness or secluded areas.

This is a good place to interject an important point. This chapter isn't just about trying to find quality hunting areas close to home. Actually, it's more about the importance of not falling into the rut of thinking that the hunting is *always* better somewhere else.

Success Demands Hard Work

Those hunters we hear and read about who manage to kill better-than-average bucks every year must have located a real "honey hole." It's either that or they're hunting an area where the bucks are just much easier to pattern and kill. Surely, if you could hunt a spot like that, your success rate would be equally as impressive. The way you see it, those hot-shot hunters aren't necessarily better at this sport than you. The reason they've been more successful is because they're hunting in areas that are far better than anything you've got access to.

I hate to be the one to burst your bubble, but the truth behind most successful trophy whitetail hunters is that, when it comes to big bucks, they have a very strict

113

Highly successful deer hunters aren't lucky. Nor do they necessaily know the location of a big buck "honey-hole." In most cases their success has come about becasue they're willing to work harder than the other hunters in the area.

work ethic. Nothing is left to chance, and nothing is taken for granted. No matter where these individuals hunt, they expend an enormous amount of time and energy learning everything they can about the area and the deer that live there.

Interestingly, this approach to the sport remains constant whether they're hunting close to home or hundreds, or even thousands, of miles away. In the simplest terms, these guys *always* apply themselves 100 percent to the task at hand. Nothing is left to chance, which is a real key to becoming a consistently successful hunter.

As most serious trophy hunters already know, scouting is a very important tool when searching out the whereabouts of a big buck. I'm not talking about a couple of half-hearted attempts at trying to find a big buck. Driving around in your car just before dark and glassing crop land isn't always an accurate way of determining the potential of the buck population. Neither is spending just a couple of hours walking in the woods.

Evaluating the true potential of any area, even those close to home, means you're going to have to spend an enormous amount of time studying every nook and cranny in the area. It's surprising how little of the available cover a big buck will use if he is forced to. Unless you stomp every foot of that cover, it's possible he could keep his presence a secret for quite some time (or possibly forever).

Nothing will increase your success rate on big bucks like becoming absolutely familiar with the areas you plan to hunt. It doesn't matter how long you've been hunting a certain spot or how knowledgeable you think you are about the area, you aren't familiar with it at all until you've walked every square inch of it. This is true even for those spots right in your back yard.

It's vitally important to locate things like bedding areas, travel corridors and food and water sources. Until you know how and why the deer are using each and every part of their range, there's a good chance the bucks will continue to elude you. Being out of position by a mere 50 yards can often be the difference between success and failure. This is especially true for bow-hunters.

Unfortunately, many deer hunters get into a rut of thinking they know all there is to know about their hunting areas. When they fail to see a big buck from their stand, they automatically assume it's because there are no big bucks around. Instead of taking the time to investigate the area more thoroughly to confirm their suspicions, they continue to hunt an unproductive stand, relying solely on luck to fill their tag.

Worse yet, they give up on the area entirely and give in to the temptation that the grass is surely greener on the other side of the fence. They move on to a new area, all the while telling themselves that the hunting has to be better in this spot. But the sad truth is this: If they don't take the time to investigate their new area, it's doubtful if it will be any better than the old one.

Don't Just Assume—Investigate

Attempting to assess the quality of an area purely on speculation is a common mistake. This is especially true of areas close to home. Perhaps we drive by the area on occasion and never notice any big buck activity. Or maybe it's one of those spots that's just too close to home to be any good. Again, we make the

Nothing will prove more beneficial to your big buck hunting efforts than gaining familiarity with the areas you're going to be hunting.

assumption that if there truly was a monster buck living in the vicinity, we surely would have seen him.

Whatever the case, remember that it's impossible to judge the potential of any area from the front seat of your vehicle. Like it or not, you have to get out in the woods and fields and do some leg work. If you don't, it's possible you might never find a big buck to hunt. This might remain true even if that animal is lurking right under your nose.

A couple of years ago, my good friend and hunting partner Paul Gumness spent most of the fall bow-hunting an area a good distance from our cabin. I can't really blame Paul for this, as he was seeing a lot of deer in the area he was hunting. Still, his efforts to bag a buck had met with nothing but failure.

Then one afternoon, just for a change of pace, Paul decided to forsake his long drive and instead sit on a stand located right behind our cabin. Less than an hour after he got settled, a dandy 8-point buck walked by at mere fifteen yards away. Unfortunately, by the time Paul got to full draw, the buck was in some thick brush and moving away. He never got a shot at the deer.

Paul went back to that same stand the next time he got a chance to hunt. About a half-hour after daylight, Paul heard something walking through the frosty oak leaves behind him. Turning his head, he saw the same buck he'd seen previously. This time, the 8-pointer stayed well out of bow range and eventually walked out of sight. My partner figured he had lost out again.

Nearly an hour later, Paul again heard the sounds of a deer walking through the frozen oak leaves. Unbelievably, the same buck he'd seen earlier was back and walking right at him. At a range of about 15 yards, the deer suddenly turned broadside. Paul came to full draw, followed the buck along for a couple of steps

116

and then released his arrow. He watched the trophy pile up in a heap after a short 60-yard dash. Interestingly, Paul could see the cabin from his stand. Talk about a backyard buck!

One of the reasons the buck was living in such close proximity to our cabin was the presence of a preferred food source (acorns). Another factor which contributed to the buck's presence was that, even though humans were close by, he had not been harassed. In addition, the 8-pointer could find an abundance of adequate cover in the woodlot. The buck's downfall also could be attributed to the fact that Paul wasn't totally unfamiliar with the area. Even though he had overlooked this spot in recent years, scouting trips in previous years had shown him exactly where his stand should be placed.

Get Out of the Car and Into Your Back Yard

A number of years ago, I also got into the habit of hunting the "other side of the fence." To begin with, I'd drive more than 100 miles just to get to my cabin in northern Wisconsin. Then I'd drive an additional 20 to 25 miles from my cabin to get to the areas I wanted to hunt. As far as I was concerned, there wasn't a buck big enough to interest me living in most of the country I was driving through to get to my hunting areas. My belief in that assumption was strong, even though I had actually done very little preliminary scouting of those areas.

Eventually, and after some prompting by a couple of hunting partners, I did some very in-depth scouting of an area I had been driving by for years. Lo and behold, I found enough significant sign to determine that a couple bruiser bucks were living somewhere in the vicinity. Unbelievably, this spot was just a mile from my cabin.

Over the course of the next four years, I shot a heavy-beamed 8-pointer, a high-racked 9-pointer and a big bodied 11-pointer all out of that one area. Without a doubt, those three bucks would have remained an untapped resource had I not taken the time to scout this spot just down the road.

Big bucks will live anywhere they can find the requirements needed to stay alive—adequate supplies of food, water and cover. A lack of hunting pressure also could be a big factor in how a trophy buck ultimately decides where he should take up residence. Sometimes, this place of residence may be your very own back yard. But regardless of where they might be located, these spots are the last places most deer hunters would think of looking for a big buck.

It's kind of like people who own a house on a lake. From what I've seen, these people seldom fish from their own dock. More times than not, they spend the majority of their time fishing some secret "hot spot" on the other side of the lake.

These individuals have spent an enormous amount of time learning every hump and piece of structure in their "honey holes." They know there are a lot of fish relating to the spot. And there's always the possibility of hooking into a real lunker. This thought alone gives these people the confidence to keep coming back to their favorite spots, even though they return home with their live wells empty most of the time.

117

This buck was living right under my nose, in an area I was routinely drinving by to get to a "better" spot.

Although this would seem to be a potentially productive pattern, it certainly isn't the only one available. Undoubtedly, the angler who jumps in his boat and heads out across the lake is passing up some excellent fishing much closer to home.

I've caught some big bass right out from under docks and boathouses, while the owners of those structures were fishing elsewhere on the lake. Believe me, big fish are not unlike big whitetails. They will live *anywhere* they can find both adequate food and cover. Unfortunately, some whitetail hunters are a lot like some fisherman. They think better hunting awaits them somewhere other than in the woods close to home.

At one time some years ago I bow-hunted a couple of areas that were located close to my home. But after several frustration-filled seasons, I gave up on those spots. I just wasn't seeing any really big bucks. Also, the average age of the bucks shot in this area during our gun-deer season was 1-1/2 years old. Only very rarely did someone kill a buck that was even close to what could be considered trophy size. I felt that if there were any number of big bucks living in the vicinity, certainly more of them should be getting killed every year.

My feelings about the aforementioned area have changed dramatically in recent years. To begin with, I've found enough evidence while scouting to convince myself that there are at least a couple of trophy size bucks living in the vicinity. And then during a recent spring scouting foray to the area, I found a tremendous set of matched shed antlers. The antlers have six typical points to a side, with four additional stickers. The gross typical score of the rack would be somewhere in the mid-160s.

But the final determining factor has come during two recent deer seasons. My brother Mike and his son Isaac have each taken monster bucks from the area I just mentioned. Isaac's deer, taken during the 1994 season, possesses a massive, long-tined 8-point rack and boasts a 20-inch inside spread. Mike's deer was equally as impressive. The buck has a basic 10-point frame with a 17-1/2-inch inside spread. The rack also sports five "sticker" points. The gross score on the 15-pointer is somewhere in the mid-160s non-typical.

This is proof positive that there are big bucks in the area. And I'm sure they've been there all along. Still, I had neglected the spot for a good many years. And only because I *assumed* there were no trophy size animals in the area. No one, including me, was seeing any big bucks. Also, darn few were being killed each year. Therefore, it seemed only logical to assume that the area had been "shot out." How wrong I was!

One very positive aspect about searching out good hunting spots closer to home is that you'll surely get more time to hunt these places. Even if you feel the area has only marginal potential for producing a big buck, stick with it. A spot that is pretty good, but that you can hunt with regularity, may be far better than a great spot that you're able to hunt only on very rare occasions.

As long as you're careful, exposure can be a great contributing factor to the success of any hunter. The more time you spend hunting, the greater your chances for connecting on a trophy deer.

My brother Mike with proof positive that the grass isn't always greener in distant hunting lands. Mike shot this 15-pointer a mere 400 yards from his house.

The basic formula for consistent success on big bucks is hard work. Mature deer are very special animals no matter where they are found. And killing one usually isn't any easier somewhere else than it is where you're currently hunting. Take it from me, those hunters you read and hear about who consistently take better than average bucks are able to do so because of their dedication to the sport. Their philosophy is the same no matter where they're hunting. They get to know the area as well as they can and then spend as much time as possible actually hunting.

And to keep their confidence level high, these guys keep one thing uppermost in their minds. The grass *isn't* necessarily greener on the other side of the fence.

Greg's Proven Pointers

- One of my greatest achievements as a deer hunter came when I was able to shrug off those feelings that the "grass is always greener" somewhere other than where I was hunting.

- Hunters seem especially susceptible to the belief that those areas closest to home are always the least productive for big bucks.

- Don't fall into the trap of trying to assess the potential of any area purely through assumption and/or speculation.

- Don't develop the attitude that big bucks are asways easier to find and kill in other areas. The basic formula for big buck success is hard work—regardless of the area!

CHAPTER ELEVEN

Staging Areas

It's not often that deer hunters are faced with the type of problem I'm about to describe. This "problem" is one I encountered some years ago while bow-hunting in my home state of Wisconsin.

The whole thing started when I discovered an alfalfa field where a number of deer were feeding on a regular basis. Interestingly, I just happened to mention the field to a friend of mine. He told me that earlier in the season he had seen several better-than-average bucks feeding in the alfalfa. Because this guy's word is usually as good as gold, I decided to check out the area a bit closer. That's when I ran into the "problem."

The alfalfa field was bordered on three sides by woods. My initial plan was to walk along the edge of the woods and check for active runways. I'd then decide which runways showed the most promise and go from there—sort of a process of elimination.

The problem was that every single runway coming to the field—and there must have been at least two dozen—showed an almost equal amount of buck sign. Never before had I run into a situation where there was *too much* buck sign. Because of this, it appeared that locating the perfect stand site was going to be an impossible task!

Past experiences of this type had taught me that I'd probably get only one chance to arrow a good buck. This meant that if I misread the existing buck sign and put my stand in the wrong place, I'd blow it. But with all the sign I'd found, how on earth was I going to decide which runway would provide me with my best opportunity at a big buck?

In most cases, staging areas are found along active rub-lines. These buck playgrounds can be great places to wait in ambush for a big deer.

Instead of giving up, I decided to try a slightly different scouting tactic—one that had been productive in the past. Moving back into the woods a couple of hundred yards, I began to slowly walk on a line that allowed me to parallel the field. When I was about halfway around the field, I found what I was looking for.

A quick glance was enough to tell me that everything about the set-up was perfect. Even with the amount of buck sign present on all the different runways, I felt as though this was the absolute best place for an ambush. I hurriedly prepared a tree for my portable stand, then quickly walked out of the area. My confidence level was very high as I drove away from the field.

A week later, on a cold and snowy late-October afternoon, I returned to hunt from the stand. Thirty minutes after getting settled, a 10-point buck walked into view. At a range of 15 yards, the big deer suddenly stopped and started rubbing his antlers on a small sapling. There wasn't an opening sufficient for me to get an arrow through, so I became a mere spectator—at least for the moment.

After spending perhaps 30 seconds rubbing his antlers, the buck must have decided it was time to head out to the alfalfa field for some chow. He started easing along a runway that would bring him to within 10 yards of my position. When he had two more steps to go to reach my narrow shooting lane, I came to full draw.

Nestling my sight pin just slightly behind his near front shoulder, I followed the 10 pointer for a couple of steps, then released an arrow. The buck went bounding off at the hit, running over small trees and bushes in his attempt to escape. A deer shot through both lungs with a razor sharp broadhead doesn't go far, however. He piled up after going 150 yards.

What was it that prompted me to place my stand exactly where I did? With all of the buck sign surrounding that field, why was I so confident that this one particular spot would be the absolute best place for my stand? Both of these questions can be answered with two words: *Staging area.*

Any deer hunter who has spent more than the "normal" amount of time in the woods undoubtedly has seen a number of staging areas. But as I've discovered, not many hunters really know the role that staging areas play in the lives of pre-rut whitetail bucks. Nor do they really know all the places where you might expect to find staging areas. Also, there are a fair number of hunters who have yet to realize the benefits of hunting these buck "playgrounds."

Most of the information in this chapter has been substantiated by many hours of research. And why did I develop such a keen interest in staging areas? That's easy. The more knowledgeable I became about this aspect of whitetail buck behavior, the more successful I became. I can state without hesitation that in the past 10 years my knowledge of staging areas is responsible for the demise of at least a half-dozen whitetail bucks.

Along with those "for sure" kills, I've also seen a good number of big bucks that walked by without offering a shot. I've also shot at and missed a few. And along the way there have been dozens of immature bucks that I've passed up. With these kinds of results, you can see why I've placed so much emphasis on hunting around staging areas.

What They Look Like and Where to Find Them

Where exactly is the best place to look for staging areas? Right along active rub-lines. Briefly, rub-lines are a series of antler rubs found along the preferred travel routes of whitetail bucks. While they're very seldom on a straight line, these series of rubs still link a very definite point A with a definite point B. (Most rub-lines occur between bedding and feeding areas.)

Somewhere between point A and point B, and right along a buck's rub-line, is where you'll find *most* staging areas. These are some of the best places to ambush a whitetail buck during the pre-rut.

What does a staging area look like? Usually, there will be a very heavy concentration of buck antler rubs in a relatively small area. It's not unusual to find a dozen severely rubbed trees in a staging area. There might even be some saplings that have been rubbed and snapped cleanly off. Big bucks are also fond of demolishing small clumps of brush. In most cases, I've also found a number of fresh scrapes in the immediate vicinity. Often, the runway(s) leading into the staging area will be very pronounced and obvious.

Common sense will tell you that there's no way the buck has made all the sign in just one or two visits. With the amount of rub and scrape activity present, it's obvious he's visiting this particular spot on a fairly regular basis.

Food Source and Bedding Staging Areas

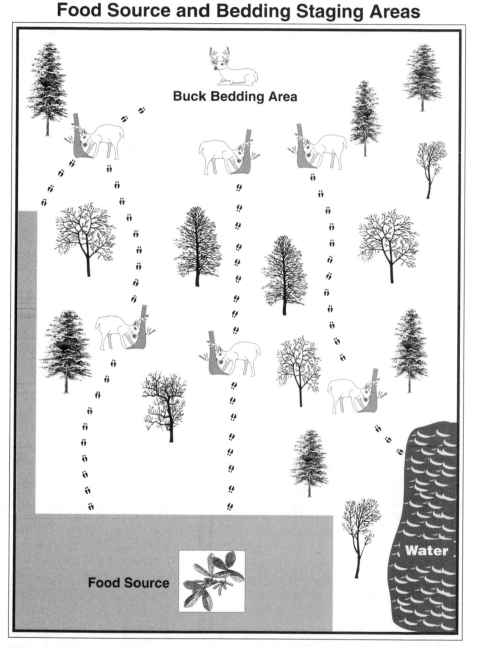

This graphic shows the location of two of the most productive types of staging areas—those found near food sources and the ones located on the very edge of buck bedding areas. Remember, daylight visits by bucks to these "playgrounds" increase as the prerut progresses. These visits all but cease, however, once breeding begins.

Staging Areas

Buck Travel Routes (Rub/Scrape-Lines)

Now that you know how to identify staging areas, it's time to discuss where along rub-lines you might find them. When I first started hunting these hot spots, I thought they were found only in the thicker brush bordering an open feeding area. This open feeding area could have been a field, a clearcut or even an open oak woodlot. However, additional research showed me that there are other places where staging areas might be found.

There are, especially in agricultural areas, places where deer have to travel across large expanses of open ground to get from one patch of cover to another. For example, I know where there is a good-sized wooded area. This patch of big buck deluxe is complete with head-high buckbrush and briars as big around as your thumb. As you might have guessed, the deer have found the woods to be an ideal bedding spot.

The thick woods is bordered on one side by a field. On the other side of the field is a relatively open oak woodlot. The deer love feeding on the acorns found in the oak woods, but they have to cross the open field to get there. This is no problem for the does, fawns and smaller bucks living in the area. In fact, they often walk across the field in broad daylight.

Such is not the case with the mature bucks, however. While these animals may arrive at the crossing point while there is still some daylight left, they usually won't cross the open ground until they can do so under the cover of darkness.

The big bucks hang back in the thick brush along the edge of the field waiting for darkness to fall. And while they're waiting, they spar, make and freshen scrapes and rub their antlers on the trees and bushes in the immediate vicinity. (This is their way of venting their frustrations and expending a bit of nervous energy.) After only a few visits to the spot the bucks will have established a very obvious and highly visible staging area.

Because of the amount of deer sign they're sure to find there, some hunters would go ahead and place their stands in the oaks. But if you want to see the mature bucks, it's fairly obvious where your stand should be placed. You should set-up either right in the staging area or on one of the runways leading to it.

In those situations where deer are walking from cover right into an open feeding area staging areas usually will be found in a slightly different location. *In most instances,* bucks will stage some distance back from the edge of the feeding area. That was the case with the buck I talked about at the beginning of this chapter. The 10-pointer was staging approximately 200 yards from the alfalfa field. I found more than 20 steaming fresh rubs and several inch-deep scrapes in a tiny clearing. This was the tip-off I needed to determine that I had found a very active and often-visited staging area.

One night during our archery season some years ago I received a phone call from an acquaintance of mine. It seems this guy was sitting on his stand when, about a half-hour before dark, a decent 8-point buck walked into view. My friend could tell almost immediately that the deer was going to stay out of bow range, so he just sat back and watched. The buck spent the next 20 minutes pretty much in one spot, rubbing his antlers on several different trees. Eventually, the deer walked off in the direction of the field.

Staging areas found near food sources can be highly productive. Take note: In most cases these staging areas will be located some distance from the edge of the food source.

"Do you think I should stay where I am and hope he walks by, or should I move over to where he was rubbing his horns," the guy asked? I strongly suggested to the fellow that he do a quick preliminary scouting job to see if the buck was utilizing a staging area. If he found a number of rubs other the ones the buck had made while he watched him, it was apparent the buck was visiting the spot routinely. If this were the case, I advised him to move his stand to a position that would allow him to cover the runway coming into the staging area.

It wasn't until well after the season had ended that I talked with the guy again. I asked how things had went the previous fall. "I took your advice and did some scouting, Greg. You were right, the buck was definitely staging in that same spot every day." he told me. "I went ahead and moved my stand, but unfortunately, I didn't get a chance to sit there."

It seems the guy was good-hearted enough to tell a friend about the set-up. On the very first afternoon his friend sat on the stand, he killed the buck that was using the staging area. Incidentally, this staging area also was located about 200 yards back from the edge of the alfalfa field.

Both of the above described situations describe an excellent place to look for staging areas in agricultural country. Namely, at crossing points and some distance back from the edge of open fields. In both instances, the staging areas will most likely be located along an active rub-line.

Because open fields and crop attraction are a rarity in wilderness areas, you'll have to look elsewhere for staging areas in this sort of a situation. A couple of the better places to look for staging areas in wilderness country would be along the edge of a newly logged or burned area and/or in the thicker brush bordering a stand of oak.

Open Ground Crossing Staging Areas

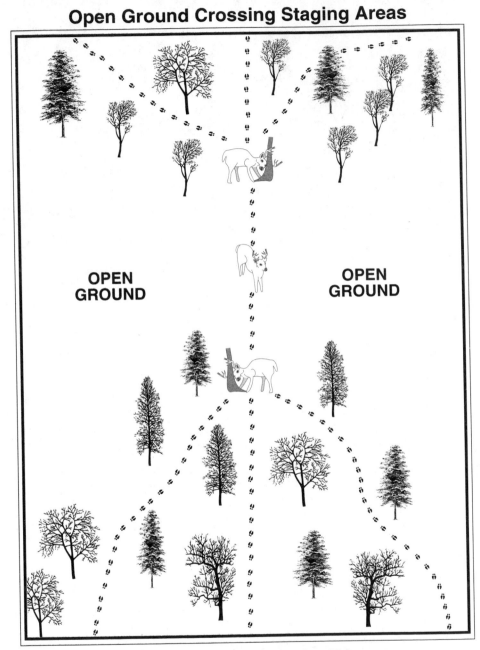

OPEN GROUND

OPEN GROUND

This illustration gives you a good indication of how bucks will establish staging areas in conjunction with open ground crossing points. Although the bucks may arrive at the crossing point while it's still light, they'll usually hesitate to cross the open ground until darkness falls. While they're waiting these deer will "work out" in the staging area. This is the spot for your stand!

Staging Areas

Buck Travel Routes (Rub/Scrape-Lines)

Bucks often hesitate before crossing a stretch of open ground. Consequently, they end up establishing staging areas near these crossing points.

Again, the pattern is similar to that found in the farm country. The does, fawns and smaller bucks might walk right out into the clearcut or oak woods in broad daylight. But the big bucks will stand back some distance in the thick cover and wait. Even during the final stages of the pre-rut, the big boys don't relish the idea of leaving the safety provided by the thicker cover. As much as the big buck would like to be out there eating and sniffing a doe or two, his instincts tell him to wait until dark before trying it.

So what do these big bucks do while they're waiting for nightfall? Just like their farmland cousins, they're going to spar, scrape, grunt, rub and literally knock the crap out of anything that gets in their way. I have both seen and heard bucks doing this in a staging area. It's quite an experience. The grunting, rubbing, scraping and brush-busting often is intended to intimidate the immature bucks that have already ventured out into the feeding area. It usually works too. I've seen smaller bucks completely vacate the area upon hearing the commotion made by the big guys.

Bedding/Staging Areas

Most of the big woods bucks I pursue are very mature animals. And the deer in the farmland areas I hunt are pressured nearly to death. Because of the nocturnal movement patterns these animals have adopted, I found I was spending far too much unproductive time in my tree stands. For the most part, the really big

Big bucks often hang back in thick cover and wait for darkness to fall before venturing into the open. While they're waiting, these deer will be rubbing and scraping.

bucks weren't arriving at the staging areas I was watching over until after dark. It was time to try something different.

I've spent years studying buck antler rubs and rub-lines. Putting my knowledge of this aspect of whitetail behavior to good use led me to discover something very interesting. Most of the big bucks I was hunting were visiting yet one more staging area. These staging areas are located on the very edges of buck bedding areas.

The first thing an undisturbed whitetail buck does after rising up out of his bed is stretch. He then stands motionless for a few minutes testing the wind and listening for anything out of the ordinary. The buck then moves a couple of steps and relieves himself. When he's finished, he once again stands motionless for a few minutes.

Then, with wind direction as his guide, the buck exits his bedding area. The big deer will make another stop on the very edge of his daytime sanctuary. This stop will be at a bedding/staging area. He'll spend a few minutes here rubbing his antlers and, in a sense, working out the kinks. After he's done rubbing, the buck will start moseying towards his final destination, whatever it may be (food, water, etc.).

The staging area that the buck just visited is the best place to try and kill a big buck. There are two reasons. First, the buck will visit this bedding/staging area almost every day during the pre-rut. And second, but more importantly, because this staging area is in such close proximity to his bedding area, there's a very good chance the buck will show up there during daylight hours.

Judging from what I've seen, staging areas located near a buck's bedroom aren't as pronounced or obvious as the staging areas found closer to food sources and crossing points. Nor are the antler rubs as large as those found elsewhere. As of yet, I have no explanation for this. My speculation is that, after rising out of his bed, the buck is only rubbing to more or less "loosen up," much like an athlete doing a bit of light exercising before an event. Also, bucks don't seem to spend quite as much time staging near their bedding areas.

As mentioned, bedding/staging areas aren't nearly as obvious as staging areas found elsewhere. Therefore, they tend to be much harder to find than the ones located at other points along a buck's rub-line. Nonetheless, they are out there, believe me. And the fact that they are hard to find isn't the only negative aspect of hunting these bedding/staging areas.

Extra Care Needed Near Bedding Areas

Setting up in such close proximity to a mature buck's bedding area can be a tricky situation. Because of this, I would suggest you conduct your searches for bedding/staging areas during the off-season. This is also the best time to find and prepare stand sites *and* to figure out approach routes that allow you to get into those stands undetected.

There are many factors that must be taken into consideration when hunting big bucks right where they sleep. The most important factor of all is wind direction. You should *never* sit on your stand if the wind is even slightly "wrong." Also, don't hesitate to abandon your stand if you feel that a switch in wind direction will betray your presence.

The best time to search for bedding/staging area stand sites is during the post-season and/ or spring. Doing so ensures that you will keep disturbances to minimum during the open season.

Stand placement in relationship to the actual bedding/staging area usually will be dictated by what you find during your scouting trips. If you feel you'll be able to set up right in the staging area, by all means do so. The closer you can get to where a buck is sleeping, the better chance you'll have of catching him moving about while there's still plenty of shooting light.

But there will be situations when it just won't be possible to set-up right in the bedding/staging area. It could be that there isn't a tree close by that's suitable for a stand site. Or maybe your scouting has shown that the buck is bedding right next to the staging area. No matter what the circumstance, there's no cause for alarm. Simply find the rub-line that leads out of the buck's bedding/staging area and set up somewhere along this route. Try to stay as close as possible to the bedding area, however.

It seems that almost all of the big bucks I've patterned have one particular spot where they prefer to bed. No matter what food source the buck is using or how far away that food source happens to be, he'll almost always return to the same bedding area after a night's wandering.

Maybe this explains why I've often found staging areas at several different points around a big buck's bedding area. Both wind direction and the location of a preferred food source may dictate just where a buck is going to exit his bedding area.

Still, most of the big bucks I've hunted had one exit point they use more than any other. This trail will be identifiable because: Number one, the trail will show much more use; and number two, the staging area found here will show much more rub activity. If you have to pick one spot to prepare for future hunting possibilities, this is the one to choose.

Just as multiple buck sightings are a strong possibility when hunting along rub-lines, so it is when near staging areas. For instance, there's a particular staging area we've been hunting for a number of years. During one season, my older brother Mike shot a buck in that staging area with his bow. A couple of weeks later, while sitting on the same stand during gun season, my younger brother Jeff shot a dandy 8-pointer. Neither one of these bucks was the huge 10-pointer I had seen in that staging area during the archery season.

The chances that several bucks are using a certain staging area is more often a rule than an exception. It doesn't take a rocket scientist to figure out that hunting such areas certainly increases your chances for success.

Hunting near staging areas can be a productive tactic during all phases of the pre-rut. And it can be especially so in that three- to five-day period just prior to the rut . But as is the case when watching over scrapes or sitting along active rub-lines, waiting in ambush near staging areas becomes just about a lost cause once breeding begins

Greg's Proven Pointers

- Most staging areas are located along active rub-lines

- Those staging areas that are established in conjunction with a nearby food source can be highly productive for big bucks.

- Hunting near staging areas is most productive during the latter stages of the pre-rut. But you need to relocate your hunting efforts closer to doe/fawn activity areas once actual breeding begins.

- Bedding/staging areas are great places to ambush mature whitetail bucks. I strongly suggest, however, that you do your scouting and stand site selection during the off-season.

CHAPTER TWELVE

Effective Clearcut Tactics

I'd bet that this chapter proves to be the most popular in this book. I base that statement on one simple fact: Just about everywhere you find whitetails in North America, you'll also find some sort of ongoing logging activity. And as most of us know, white-tailed deer relate big-time to cut areas.

But merely being aware of the above-mentioned information doesn't necessarily ensure success. Before they'll ever be able to develop effective strategies for hunting in and around clearcuts, hunters must first understand how whitetails use and relate to these places.

Admittedly, clearcuts are an eyesore and a good reason for feeling depressed—at least initially. But those of us who are "in the know" are aware of the tremendous deer hunting that will soon be found in and around cut areas. This tremendous hunting is because of the fact that clearcuts create an instant attraction for whitetails. That attraction is an abundance of the most-preferred browse-type deer foods.

Concentrating your efforts around browse areas can be beneficial regardless of what type of environment you're hunting. However, it's really an asset for those of us who hunt whitetails in big woods. This is because, in most big woods environments, there are no crop attractants. As I've become fond of telling novice big-woods hunters, the biggest step toward achieving consistent success is first learning exactly what the deer are eating. After that, everything else sort of falls into place.

As I said, it doesn't matter what sort of habitat you're hunting. If there has been some recent logging activity, the deer will utilize that logged area. This is because, starting the second a felled tree hits the ground, a new, highly preferred food source is suddenly available. Discarded tree-tops provide deer with succu-

Discarded tree-tops provide deer with a new, highly desirable food source. So from the first second that a felled tree hits the ground, logging activity begins to concentrate deer.

lent and tender browse-type food that, up until the trees were cut down, was unavailable. Now that those trees are laying on the ground, the deer in the area are going to utilize them. In most cases, the discarded tops will hold the deer over until substantial re-growth develops.

To develop effective strategies for hunting clearcuts, it's important hunters first know how whitetails relate to different age-class cuts. Believe me, there's a world of difference between the way a mature buck utilizes a first-year cut area and the way he uses a five-year-old cut. There also comes a point in time when whitetails will just about quit using a cut area.

First-Year Cuts

Some hunters have the impression that first-year cuts are of relatively little value to whitetails—or to hunters. Therefore, many people overlook such areas. What a mistake! A *great deal* of my clearcut hunting effort revolves around first-year cut areas.

Not all first-year cuts are equally attractive. Hunters can expect to see the most whitetail activity around those places that were cut sometime during the previous winter or early spring. The reason for this is simple. Mature, wide-canopied trees block sunlight and rob valuable moisture from small trees and plant life. Once those trees are removed, however, grasses, weeds, underbrush and tree saplings grow back quite quickly. But the re-growth will be thickest and most succulent

135

Although first-year clearcuts don't provide much in the way of cover, they do provide deer with an almost unlimited supply of weeds, grasses and preferred browse-type foods.

after being exposed to the summer sun and rains. (Years of observation have shown me that whitetails consider every bit of the aforementioned re-growth to be highly delectable.)

So it's obvious that whitetails will utilize the re-growth in a first-year clearcut as a main source of food. But there's another important fact that hunters will quickly notice about first year clearcuts. Although there's an abundance of food to be found, such places offer very little, if any, suitable cover for the deer. So while the deer will concentrate heavily on the cut for food, they will have to search elsewhere for bedding areas.

I think this is why so many hunters harbor negative opinions about first-year cuts. Just one look at a fresh clearcut will tell you it's highly unlikely you'll catch a big buck in such a spot during daylight. In fact, the only deer you'll probably see in the cut are the does, fawns and small bucks that reside in the area.

But just because you aren't seeing any big bucks near a first-year cut doesn't mean they aren't frequenting the spot. I can almost guarantee they will be. Better yet—provided hunting pressure isn't too heavy—those bucks will get into fairly predictable movement patterns. They'll leave their bedding areas and make their way to the clearcut sometime before dark in late afternoon. Then they'll head out of the cut at first light in the morning. I'm sure most deer hunters realize that any time deer get into such predictable patterns, success rates can rise dramatically.

The best way I know of to figure out how deer are approaching and departing a first year cut is by walking all the way around the outside perimeter of the cut area.

Hunting First-Year Clearcuts

Although first-year clearcuts provide deer with an abundance of highly preferred foods, they don't offer much in the way of cover. Hence, you'll have to find out where the deer are bedding and how they are approaching the cut area. Personally, I've witnessed a lot of buck action while hunting along points of standing timber that jut out into first year clearcuts.

Gun Hunting Stand Sites

Bow Hunting Stand Sites

Buck Travel Routes (Rub/Scrape-Lines)

Although you should pay attention to every active runway you find, your Number One priority is to seek out runways that show evidence of buck travel. These runways should be fairly easy to identify because of the presence of scrapes and antler rubs. Because I prefer to hunt for mature bucks, I'll search out and establish stand sites along buck travel routes where I find the largest antler rubs.

If the areas you hunt experience a lot of pressure, then I doubt you'll catch a mature buck near a first year clearcut during daylight—at least for most of the season. For this reason, you'd be wise to follow known buck travel routes some distance away from the cut before looking for stand sites. How far is far enough? Because each situation is bound to be at least slightly different, there's no standard answer to that question.

What I like to do is start out by placing my stands a couple of hundred yards from the cut. If I don't see any daylight buck activity after a couple of hunts, I'll move a bit farther away from the cut. I'll keep doing this until I witness some buck movement. Some of the most productive gun and bow stands I've ever had were located on buck travel routes that linked bedding areas to first-year clearcuts.

However, there is one time during the season when I will place my stands right on the very edges of first-year cuts—during the peak of the rut. At this time of year it's not unusual to see big bucks cruising the outside edges of cut areas in broad daylight. What they're doing is cross-checking runways the antlerless deer are using to enter and exit the cut. Somehow, mature bucks know this is the quickest and most effective way of scent-checking a specific area. To our benefit, it's a pattern we are able to take advantage of.

Two- to Ten-Year-Old Cuts

Clearcuts in this age-class are the ultimate white-tailed deer havens. Not only do the cuts offer deer an abundance of the most-nutritious foods, they also provide them with the exact type of cover they prefer for bedding and covert travel. This situation poses a unique problem for hunters, however.

While the deer were forced to bed in outlying areas before, they can now literally stand up out of their beds and start feeding. The problem with this is that the deer have absolutely no reason to leave the cut. And because visibility in relatively new cuts is only slightly more than a few feet, your chances of shooting a buck while hunting from the ground are just about zero.

I use a very basic approach for searching out potentially productive stand sites near these cuts. Standing back some distance, I visually scan the area, trying to locate spots that demand a closer look.

Features that catch my eye include points of standing timber that extend into the cut, and ridges or hills in the cut. Deer love to use the points of timber as main travel routes when exiting and entering the cut. And the elevated pieces of ground can serve deer as both prime bedding spots and places from which they're able to observe the surrounding area.

Any bucks living in the cut will, at one time or another, use every point of standing timber in a cut. This means most likely you will find evidence of buck

Once clearcuts reach this age-class, they provide deer with the type of security cover they require for both bedding and covert travel.

activity on every point you scout. I prefer to concentrate the majority of my hunting efforts on those points that show the greatest amount of mature buck sign. As I've so often stated, I consider large antler rubs to be the most conclusive evidence of big buck presence.

While I might have shunned the idea of placing my stands on the very edge of first-year cuts, I no longer adhere to this rule. The bucks are now bedding right in the cut area, which means this is the best place to try to catch an antlered animal moving around during legal shooting times.

Because the re-growth is now at the stage where visibility at ground level is severely restricted, you have no choice but to hunt from an elevated position. A tactic I've found most effective is to place my stands in trees located on the very tips of timbered points. Being in such a position gives me the luxury of covering a specific buck travel route on the point itself. However, I can also see out into and cover a bit of the cut area.

There are a couple of factors that dictate how high I place my stands. The primary factor is the height of the re-growth in the cut. Obviously, the taller the re-growth is, the higher you'll have to go to see out into the cut.

The other factor that has a bearing on treestand height is the type of weapon I'm hunting with. When hunting with bow and arrow, I usually put my treestand just high enough to allow me to cover to the limits of my effective range. In most cases, I'm able to accomplish this by getting 15 to 20 feet off the ground.

It's a different story, however, when I'm hunting with my trusty .270. I want to get high enough so that I can see several hundred yards out into a cut. Also, I want to ensure that I'll have a fairly clear shot at any bucks I see at that distance. To accomplish this I've found it's imperative that my stands be placed a good distance off the ground.

During our gun season several years ago I hunted a three-year-old cut that was holding a large number of deer. From the ground, it was impossible to see more than 20 yards in the cut. To overcome this problem, I placed my portable stand 30 feet up in a tree located on the very tip of a wooded point. Not only did this substantially increase visibility, it also gave me a relatively clear field of fire well out into the cut. I killed a very respectable 8-point buck the second time I sat on the stand.

I mentioned that whitetails often use ridges/hills in cuts as bedding areas. This, of course, makes these excellent stand site spots. But just like any other place where whitetails are sleeping, you must take great care when hunting these bedding area stands. Because the deer are laying on an elevated piece of ground, it's going to be nearly impossible to approach them without being seen.

What I would suggest is that you use these bedroom stands for morning hunts only. To realize any sort of success, you'll have to be at your stands *before* the deer arrive back at their bedding area. And the only way you'll be able to accomplish this is by walking into your stand sites some time before daylight. Hopefully, a "shooter" buck will make the mistake of walking within range.

Another potential hotspot in cut areas are those "islands" of trees left behind by loggers. I've seen examples where an island consisted of no more than a dozen trees. On the other hand, I've seen islands that exceeded 10 acres in size. While

The height of the re-growth in a cut area can have a direct bearing on how high you place your tree stands. When bowhunting right in a 2- to-10-year-old clearcut, I'll put my stands at a height that allows me to cover out to the limits of my effective range.

whitetails will relate to islands of any size, it takes only a bit of common sense to see that you'll stand a better chance for success by hunting the larger islands.

Islands can provide whitetails with more than enough of the cover they desire for bedding and safe travel—even in the year(s) before the cut grows to a height that will afford good cover. Interestingly, in the North, these islands usually are covered with oak trees. Of course, this means that in years when acorns are plentiful, the magnetic effect of the islands is enhanced even more.

Just like when hunting points of timber, I prefer to place my stands in a tree somewhere along the edges when hunting bedding areas or islands. Doing so allows me to not only to see and cover part of the bedding areas/islands, but I'll also be able to look out into and cover a portion of the cuts. Again, how high I place my stands is dependent upon the height of the re-growth and whether I'm hunting with bow or gun.

There is yet one more place hunters should check for signs of deer activity in cuts. This is on the roads the loggers used to skid their logs to landings. In some cases, state foresters require logging contractors to seed the skidder trails in clover after logging activities have ceased in the area.

This is one situation where it's entirely possible to shoot a buck in a cut while hunting from the ground. In fact, setting up ground blinds within range of a clover-covered road can be a highly effective tactic. Also, because you can sneak along these roads without making a sound, still-hunting is another option. And don't think that this tactic will be productive only in early morning/late afternoon. Because these roads often snake through the thickest areas in a cut, it's not unusual to catch deer feeding on them during midday hours.

I've discovered another very interesting fact about the way big bucks sometimes relate to 2- to 10-year-old clearcuts. Yes, they spend a great deal of time sleeping, feeding and traveling in re-growth areas of this age-class. And they use these areas as sanctuaries to escape hunting pressure outside the cut. However, big bucks are quick to abandon these sanctuaries when threatened with pressure from within. An experience our hunting group had with a big buck nearly 20 years ago comes to mind.

Our group was making a well-organized drive through a six-year-old re-growth area. About halfway through the drive, we jumped a big buck. However, instead of playing by the rules and running past one of our standers, the buck circled around and ran out the back of the drive. (One of the drivers got a glimpse of the deer sneaking by him.) After finishing the drive, we talked it over and decided to go after the buck. With about four inches of fresh snow on the ground, we knew we'd have ideal tracking conditions. As it worked out, my dad volunteered to track the buck, while the rest of us would post along known buck crossings.

Anyway, while he was in hot pursuit of the big buck, my dad noticed something very interesting. The more pressure he put on the deer, the more he tended to stay away from thick re-growth or "slashed" areas. Yes, he would go into the re-growth, but only for a very short distance. Then he'd head right back out into the more open hardwoods. Unfortunately, all our standers (myself included) were under the impression the buck would surely stick close to the thick cover provided by the re-growth. We never did get into position to ambush that deer.

Hunting 2- to 10-Year Old Clearcuts

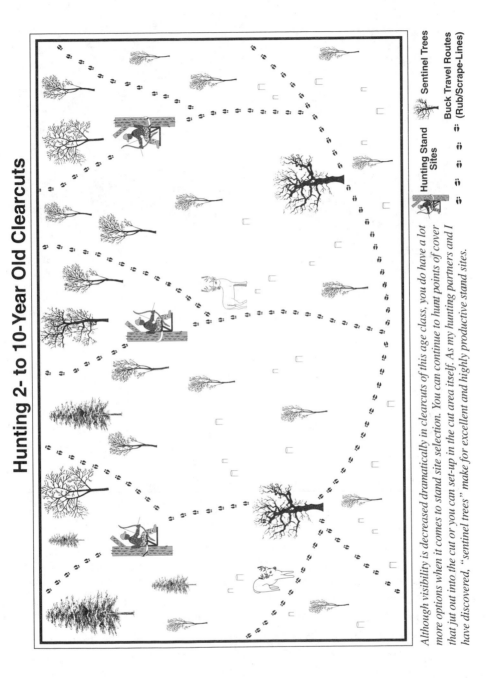

Hunting Stand Sites

Sentinel Trees

Buck Travel Routes (Rub/Scrape-Lines)

Although visibility is decreased dramatically in clearcuts of this age class, you do have a lot more options when it comes to stand site selection. You can continue to hunt points of cover that jut out into the cut or you can set-up in the cut area itself. As my hunting partners and I have discovered, "sentinel trees" make for excellent and highly productive stand sites.

143

Observations have shown me that, when pressured by several hunters, big bucks often avoid thick re-growth areas, probably because their visibility is severely limited in such places.

I've seen big bucks display this same sort of behavior several times since. It's my belief that this is because, when being pressured, most mature bucks would prefer to have as much visibility as possible. Common sense suggests that the *last* place they'll be able to realize great visibility would be in a thick re-growth area. So while they will bed, feed and travel about in 2- to 10-year-old clearcuts, big bucks seem to quickly vacate these areas when the heat is on.

Clearcuts Ten-Years-Old and Older

Clearcuts lose much of their appeal to deer when they reach the age of 10. From what I've been able to determine, there are a couple of distinct reasons for this. First of all, once the re-growth reaches a certain height, it no longer provides deer with the tender browse they desire. And second, the foliage on the new growth often becomes so thick and impenetrable, it chokes out all underbrush. The forest floor then takes on an almost parklike appearance, which means there's hardly enough cover for bedding or safe travel. One of the biggest mistake I've seen hunters make is that they continue to hunt around cuts long after those areas are no longer attractive to deer.

Throughout this article I've talked about clearcuts. I'm sure the mental image most people get when they hear the word "clearcut" is one where every single

Whitetails relate quite strongly to "sentinel trees," meaning that these trees can be great stand-site locations.

tree in a specific area has been mowed down. However, that's hardly ever the case. At least it hasn't been in the logged areas I've hunted. Provided that the log gers have followed some practical guidelines, they'll usually leave a certain number of trees standing. These "sentinel" trees as I've come to call them, have played a huge role in our success rate on whitetail bucks.

In most of the logged areas I've hunted, the trees that were left uncut have been large pine. But I've also seen cases where the uncut trees happened to be large oak or ash. However, it really doesn't matter just what species of tree it is. If it's one of only a select few trees that have been left standing, I can just about guarantee that any deer frequenting the clearcut will eventually relate to that tree.

My brother, Mike, was the first of our group to take advantage of this very consistent aspect of deer behavior. Starting in the mid-1970s, Mike reeled off an impressive record of 11 bucks in as many gun seasons while hunting from a big old pine that loggers had left standing in a huge clearcut. At the time, we were under the impression that the pine just happened to be situated in the perfect spot. However, after paying close attention to many similar situations since those days, we now know it was more a case of the deer having changed their travel patterns so they could relate to that tree.

In those parts of the country that experience deep snows during the winter months, white-tailed deer have a tendency to relate to large pine trees. The deer frequent these spots simply because it's one place (other than roads or snowmobile trails) where they can find a bit of respite from the deep snows. Until you've actu-

145

ally witnessed it for yourself, it's hard to comprehend just how much time deer will spend under the pines. While scouting and looking for shed antlers in the spring, I've seen cases where there were so many piles of deer droppings under sentinel pines that it bordered on unbelievable. It's obvious the deer that wintered in the area spent a huge amount of time under those pines. (Of course, because they spend so much time here, these are great places to look for shed antlers.)

Actually, I believe that whitetails first start relating to these sentinel trees long before the areas are initially clearcut. They then continue to relate to the trees for many years after. The importance of this to us as hunters is that the deer will have established often-used travel routes that link one sentinel tree to the next. Whenever I scout any clearcut, regardless of how old that cut might be, my first move is to check out the area immediately around any and all sentinel trees.

The next time you scout a 2- to 10-year-old clear cut area, I suggest you check out any large trees that were left standing by the loggers. I'd be willing to bet that you'll find several well-traveled runways passing almost directly underneath every sentinel tree. I'd also be willing to bet that, although those runways might have been there before the area was cut, the deer have started using them even more since the cutting took place. By placing a portable stand in one of these sentinel trees, you'll be able to cover the runways that pass directly under that tree and quite a bit of the surrounding area as well. It's a tactic my hunting partners and I have used to take scores of bucks over the years.

Much of the information in this chapter is dependent upon certain elements remaining constant from year to year. For example, weather conditions can play a significant role in how quickly (or slowly) a cut area grows back. Several consecutive years of extremely dry or wet weather can have a dramatic effect on the growth rate.

Also, deer hunters living in the southern U.S. certainly will have to adjust the growth rate figures I've presented for clearcut areas. Obviously, a 5-year-old clearcut in North Carolina or Georgia is going to have much taller and heavier vegetation than a clearcut area of the same age in Wisconsin or Michigan.

The high demand for paper products in recent years has meant a steady increase in the amount of logging activity all across this continent. Those of us who hunt for deer on public lands have especially felt the brunt of these increased logging practices.

It can be a bit frustrating and even depressing to find out your favorite deer woods has been clearcut. But in the long run, the cutting of trees usually winds up being in the best interest of both you and the deer. Hopefully, the information I've presented in this chapter will help you take advantage of this situation.

Greg's Proven Pointers

- It's a fact! Logging is a widespread practice across North America. Hence, deer hunters everywhere would be well-served to increase their knowledge of clearcut hunting strategies.

- While first-year clearcuts don't offer deer much in the way of cover, they do provide an almost unlimited supply of highly desirable foods.

- Deer can find both an abundance of cover and plentiful supplies of food in two to ten year-old clearcuts. In many cases when dealing with clearcuts of this age-class, your best strategy is to go in after'em.

- Big bucks love to bed and feed in two to ten year old clearcuts. But they will quickly abandon these places when a hunter gets on their trail.

- Sentinel trees are virtual deer magnets, regardless of the age of the clearcut. This makes them ideal places for stand sites.

CHAPTER THIRTEEN

Sneaking and Peeking

If my observations over the past several years are accurate, there are two basic strategies that gun-hunters use more than any other. One of these strategies entails establishing stand sites along known escape routes. Hunters who employ this tactic are hopeful that the encroachment of other hunters into a specific area will "push" a buck past their position.

But perhaps the most popular and widely used gun-hunting strategy, especially later in the season, is gang-driving for deer. A gang-drive consists of having a fairly large number of hunters walk through a patch of deer cover to attempt to flush any bucks that might be hiding in that cover. Somewhere up ahead more hunters are waiting in ambush. These individuals are posted along routes they hope an escaping buck might use while fleeing from the drivers.

I'm not going to argue that these tactics aren't effective. In fact, if used at the right time and executed properly, both can be highly productive ways for taking big bucks. Unfortunately, one of these tactics (sitting along escape routes) is too often used at the wrong times, and the other (gang-driving deer) is seldom executed properly.

The strategy of setting up along buck escape routes is most effective on the opening day of the season. After that, most mature bucks alter their patterns and behavior accordingly. It's highly unlikely they're going to get caught in a position where they might be jeopardizing their safety—like using an escape route. Still, I know quite a few hunters who continue to hunt opening day escape route stands well into the season. Bad move!

Hunting along buck escape routes is a great opening day tactic. However, the effectiveness of this tactic goes down significantly once opening day is history.

The sneak-and-peek method of hunting works best in terrain that provides you with fairly good visiblity.

I know very few gang-driving groups that take mature bucks on a regular basis. The main reason for this is that far too many gang-drivers simply don't execute their strategies properly. In most cases, the bucks in the drive area are fully aware of what's going on long before the drive ever starts. They know exactly where the drivers are going to walk. They also know exactly where the standers are positioned. Under these circumstances, it's highly unlikely you'll get a big buck to go where you want him to.

These are only a couple of reasons why I've grown so fond of yet another method to use when gun-hunting trophy white-tailed deer: sneaking and peeking.

What is Sneaking and Peeking?

Just what is the sneak-and-peek method? Actually, it's a hyped-up version of still-hunting. But even though the sneak-and-peek method entails covering quite a bit of ground in a relatively short period of time, you can't allow your movements to become random and careless. When sneaking, it's imperative you learn how to use both topographical and natural features to hide your movements. And when peeking, you've got to quickly figure out exactly which vantage points will allow you the best visibility.

This strategy can be a very effective way of getting within gun-range of big whitetail bucks *after* opening day. More importantly, however, you're able to accomplish this without having to rely on other hunters to "move" deer for you.

There's yet another reason why I prefer to sneak and peek when gun-hunting. In a nutshell, I've found this to be an effective tactic just about everywhere I've hunted for trophy whitetails. For instance, a big 10-point Texas whitetail fell victim to the tactic several years ago. A couple of years earlier, guide Shane Hansen and I sneaked and peeked our way to a 150-class, 11-point Alberta monster. And then there was that long-tined Montana 8-pointer…

Still, I must be completely honest. The *main* reason I find the sneak and peek method so alluring is the fact that it allows me time off from my normal hunting mode. Although I spend a certain amount of time each year gun-hunting for whitetails, bow-hunting for big bucks is my Number One passion. And as most bow-hunters will attest, the most effective way to hunt mature bucks is to sit on portable tree stands placed along the preferred travel routes of those deer.

Well folks, after spending hundreds of hours throughout the fall sitting motionless on rather small and highly uncomfortable tree stands, a change in hunting styles is very welcome indeed. The sneak-and-peek method has proven to be just what the doctor ordered. Not only does sneaking and peeking offer me a respite from sitting in a tree stand, I'm convinced that employing the tactic can instantly put me in strong contention for a chance at a good buck—anytime and anywhere!

Several years ago my good friend and fellow whitetail enthusiast Gary Clancy took a fine whitetail buck while he and I were hunting near Pine Mountain, Georgia. Gary shot the 130-class 9-pointer while employing the sneak-and-peek method I've been talking about.

Initially, Gary had been hunting from a tree stand situated between a large expanse of mature oaks and a thick patch of pines. Between daylight and about 8 a.m., he saw quite a few deer exit the oaks and head for the pines. But then the activity ceased.

A light rain had been falling all morning, so the day really hadn't brightened up yet. Because of this, Gary figured there might still be some deer hanging back in the oaks, feeding on acorns. He decided to climb down and see if he could substantiate his suspicions.

As luck would have it, a large ridge ran right through the middle of the oak forest. Using wind direction as his guide, Gary began walking along the back side of the ridge. Every so often, he'd sneak to the top and slowly peek over. Judging from the number of deer he was seeing, Gary knew he'd hit on the perfect tactic.

About an hour into his sneak-and-peek hunt, Gary slowly made his way to the top of the ridge and peeked over yet one more time. Directly below him stood a small 7-point buck. My friend quickly noticed that the little buck was peering intently down the hill. Following the deer's line of sight, Gary immediately spotted a mature doe. There was a slight flicker of motion below the doe and a then a large-racked buck walked into view. Gary saw enough to ascertain that this second buck was a definite shooter. Slowly, so as not to spook the 7-pointer, my friend brought his scoped .25-06 to his shoulder and dropped the big deer in its tracks.

I had an experience similar to Gary's during a recent gun season for deer in my home state of Wisconsin. Like Gary, I was sneaking along the back side of a

151

After spending almost all my time during archery season perched in a tree stands, I'm ready for a change of pace. Sneaking and peeking is the perfect remedy.

steep ridge, occasionally walking up and peeking over the top of the ridge. After nearly an hour of this, I had yet to see my first deer.

With about 20 minutes of legal shooting time remaining, I climbed the ridge yet one more time and slowly peeked over. Nothing. Because the ridge sort of petered out at that point, it didn't pay to go any farther. I decided to stay where I was and watch the area below until legal shooting time expired. As I soon found out, this was a very wise decision!

Less than 30 seconds after taking up my vigil, I heard a loud crash. Then a large-racked buck was running broadside through some thick brush approximately 100 yards below me. I quickly found the big deer in my scope, but with the way he was alternately popping into and out of sight, making an accurate shot was out of the question. All I could do was follow him along and hope he stopped.

If ever there was a case of luck being on my side, this was it! Just before disappearing behind a thick clump of tag alder, the buck suddenly slammed on his

Sneaking and Peaking Ridgelines

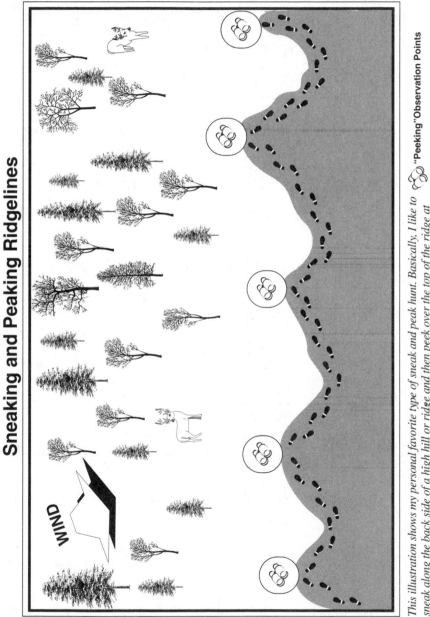

WIND

"Peeking" Observation Points

Path of Hunter

This illustration shows my personal favorite type of sneak and peak hunt. Basically, I like to sneak along the back side of a high hill or ridge and then peek over the top of the ridge at strategic points and check for deer activity below. Remember this will work only if you keep the wind direction in your favor.

brakes. Amazingly, he had stopped in a spot that afforded me a wide-open shot. A 130-grain bullet from my .270 zipped across the 150 yards that separated me from the deer. Minutes later, I was kneeling next to the dead buck, admiring his wide-spreading and heavy 9-point rack.

The above two experiences point out the best way to use the sneak-and-peak method in hilly country. First and foremost, you must keep the wind in your favor. Ideally, it should be blowing into your face when you peek over the hill-top. However, it's also okay to hunt with a slightly quartering wind.

Second, when sneaking, stay far enough down from the top of the hill so that any animals on the opposite side of the hill won't hear you. And third, use a bit of forethought when selecting your peeking spots. Look for spots that offer you rel-atively unobstructed visibility, yet offer enough cover for you to remain hidden when you peek over.

Sneaking and Peeking in Farm Country

Areas that are made up of mixed crop and forest-land also are excellent places to employ the sneak-and-peek tactic. And it really doesn't matter whether the country is comprised of large tracts of timber that butt up to crop-land or a series of smaller woodlots that are nearly surrounded by open fields. Your plan of attack remains the same.

Basically, what you want to do is sneak along just inside the edge of the woods. Every so often, and from locations that allow you to remain somewhat hidden, slip to the very edge of the woodline and peek out into the open ground and check for signs of deer activity.

During the past five years or so, I've hunted whitetails in several areas where the habitat consisted of relatively small woodlots. In many of these small wood-lot situations, fencelines linked one piece of cover to the next. Interestingly, these fencelines often were enveloped by extremely thick brush.

I've found that I'm able to retain a covert line of travel simply by following these brushy fencelines from one woodlot to the next. Also, anytime I notice a slight open-ing in the fenceline, I'll stop and take a quick peek into the field on the other side.

I'm sure some would argue that placing a stand near an open field(s) is equally as effective as sneaking and peeking. I firmly disagree. Remember, if you've got a stand set up in a position to watch a certain field or fields, you're committed to watching that particular area. This means you're actually watching a very small portion of the total amount of open land in the area. Sneaking and peeking affords you the opportunity to check for the presence of deer in a much larger part of that same area.

Sneaking and peeking also can be productive in relatively flat country. I can personally think of many areas in Canada, as well as a number of Midwestern states, that fall into this category. The only criteria you must follow when hunting such country is that there must be adequate cover for you to remain hidden while moving from one peeking spot to another.

I shot this buck while sneaking along the top of a high ridge and peeking down into a thick creek bottom.

You can use slight depressions, brushy fencerows, stands of trees, patches of brush and any other available natural obstacles, both to break up your outline and hide your movements. And when you decide to stop for a look around, make sure your vantage point affords excellent visibility while still providing enough cover for you to remain hidden.

When and Where to Sneak and Peak

The best time of day to employ the sneak-and-peak method is during the first hour or two of morning light and the last hour of daylight in late afternoon. As everyone knows, these are usually peak movement times for whitetails, which means you stand a much better chance of catching a buck out away from the security of his bedding area.

Sneaking and Peaking Farmland Edges

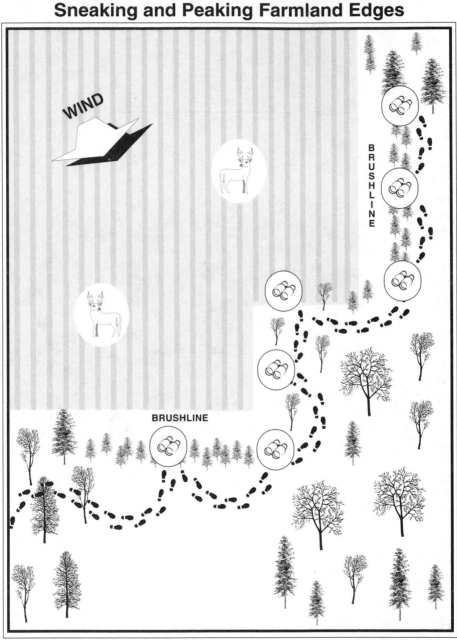

It's entirely possible to use the sneak and peek strategy in farmland/open country. The key here to use natural obstructions, such as brush lines and small woodlots to hide your movements. It also bears mentioning that sneaking and peeking in this kind of terrain is most effective during the early morning and late afternoon hours.

"Peeking" Observation Points

Path of Hunter

If you live on a part of the continent where the gun-season is open during the height of the breeding season, I strongly suggest giving the sneak-and-peek method a try. While I agree that stand-hunting can be a very productive way of taking mature whitetails, there are times when sitting in one place can leave you completely out of the game. During the peak of the rut, it's not unusual for this "deer-less" trend to continue for days.

How could such a thing happen? Easy. If the bucks that normally reside in your hunting area have been lured miles away by a couple of sweet-smelling does, then I'm afraid you don't have much chance of killing those deer from your original stand sites. This is why I maintain that sneaking and peeking might be more productive than sitting in a stand during the most aggressive part of the breeding season.

If you're willing to climb down and carefully cover some ground, there's a good chance you'll eventually discover where the most hectic breeding activity is aking place. Once you locate a concentration of deer, then it's time to get into a real sneak and peak mode.

But remember, even though the bucks might be caught up in the frenzy of full rut, they aren't necessarily careless. You still need to worry about keeping a low-profile, but I suggest moving quickly from one vantage point to another. The reason for the quick pace is that this will allow you to cover a lot more ground during a day's time. Simply put, the more ground you cover, the greater your chances of connecting on a buck.

The gun-season for deer in my home state of Wisconsin traditionally occurs during the post-rut period. But even with the tough conditions that exist during this time frame, I have managed to take a number of big bucks over the years. Interestingly, quite a few of these deer were shot while I was sneaking and peeking.

The key to achieving success on post-rut, sneak-and-peek hunts is pinpointing the exact location of highly nutritious deer foods. But it goes further. If your goal is to shoot a mature buck, then you must try to find some "hidden" food sources. In agricultural areas, look for crop attractants that lay a good distance from roads or ones that are pretty much surrounded by woods. When chasing big woods whitetails, I concentrate my sneak and peek activities around remote clearcuts, isolated oak ridges and known browse areas.

What I like to do is sneak and peek my way around the outside perimeter of these hidden feeding areas right at first light in the morning and/or during the last hour of legal shooting time in the afternoon. And because I'm dealing with animals that are already displaying very reclusive tendencies, I'm extremely careful about keeping a low profile.

How Long is Long Enough?

How long should you spend "peeking" from each vantage point? Well, that depends entirely on the situation. For instance, in areas where you can see great distances, there's really no need to spend more than a minute or so looking. In fact, a quick, 15- to 30-second scanning job should be sufficient. But at other times, you'll want to spend just a bit more time looking and watching.

Because big bucks are notorious for moving around during low-light, sneaking and peeking is most effective during the early morning and late afternoon.

On occasion, I've sat and watched from a particular vantage point for 10 minutes or more. Maybe there's just something about the spot that makes me think a buck could pop into view any second. Another thing that could keep me in one place so long is the presence of antlerless deer. I'm going to take the time to make darn sure there are no big bucks hanging around those does and fawns before I move on. This becomes doubly important during the peak breeding period.

I remember an incident where waiting just a bit longer paid off with a chance at a nice buck. The expanse of cover I was hunting on the day in question is made up of a series of fairly steep ridges that break rapidly up and away from a wide, swiftly flowing creek. All the birch and poplar had been logged out of the area 10 years earlier. The resulting re-growth not only provided plentiful browse-type foods for the deer, it also gave them excellent cover.

But while the hillsides and valleys had grown back in extremely thick brush, most of the ridge-tops were still covered with large oak and pine, which the loggers are required to leave. This made for an ideal sneak-and-peak setup.

On the day of my hunt, we were experiencing an early winter snowstorm. Nearly six inches of wind-driven snow already lay on the ground, which provided me with excellent visibility. Also, the windy conditions ensured my passage along the ridge would be relatively silent.

Sneaking and peeking is merely a hyped-up version of still-hunting. To our advantage, this tactic can prove effective just about everywhere whitetails are found.

Basically, what I did was sneak along the back side of a high, wooded ridge that paralleled the creek. Occasionally, I would make my way to the top of the ridge, peak over, check the hillside directly below me and also look down into the creek bottom. I would spend a minute or so looking and watching, then I'd drop back over the ridge, walk rather quickly another 50 to 75 yards, then sneak back to the top of the ridge and peak over again.

After about an hour of this, I made my way to the top of one particularly high ridge and peeked over. There were no deer in sight, but for some reason, I just felt like this spot should be holding some animals. Because of this feeling, I stayed put for nearly 10 minutes, intently watching the bottoms below.

All the while I stood there, the blowing snow was hitting me squarely in the face. I had just finished wiping my watering eyes with my handkerchief and was turning to leave when a slight flicker of movement caught my eye. My attention was immediately drawn to the spot.

At first I saw nothing. Then seemingly out of nowhere two whitetail bucks suddenly materialized! Obviously, the bucks had been bedded there the whole time. The falling snow had done a nice job of providing them with some natural camouflage. The bucks would have went unseen, had they not decided to stand up out of their beds.

Quickly, I dropped to one knee, flipped off my scope covers and put the crosshairs on the bigger of the two deer. The bucks were standing well down into the bottoms, at least 200 yards away. I waited until the wind velocity decreased a slight bit, got as steady as possible and sent a bullet speeding across the valley. I found the thick-necked eight pointer piled up 100 yards from where he had been standing when I shot. (By the way, the fact that the two bucks were laying side by side was proof-positive of a post-rut situation.)

Other Factors for Success

Ideally, the sneak-and-peek approach works best when your footfalls can't be heard by the deer. A little bit of wind, snow cover or wet ground make for the best sneaking conditions. Unless I've got a rather large ridge or hill to block the sounds of my foot-steps, I won't even attempt to use the sneak-and-peek method during extremely dry, noisy conditions.

Another thing I've found is that a good set of binoculars is a must when sneaking and peeking. Believe me, you DON'T want to be using your rifle-scope to glass likely looking spots or to check out possible targets. Doing the former can cause incredible eye strain, while the latter isn't a safe practice.

In case you haven't guessed, I'm not a big fan of the still-hunting method for taking trophy whitetails. The biggest rap I have against still-hunting is the basic philosophy of the tactic itself. Aficionados of still-hunting claim that the key to success is moving at a pace that puts a snail to shame. I've actually heard some hunters make the claim that it sometimes takes them an hour to go a mere 100 yards.

To me, it's absolutely ridiculous to move along at a pace that allows you to cover only a hundred yards in an hour's time. Why? That's easy. Even proponents of still-hunting have to admit that, provided you climbed high enough, you'd probably be able to cover all of that same 100 yards from a tree stand. Undoubtedly, you'd also have a much better field of fire than if you were standing on the ground. So why not put up a tree stand, sit on it for an hour, then move 100 yards? Or better yet, why not do a sneak-and-peek hunt through the area.

I've become fond of saying that, when one takes up the pursuit of trophy animals, it's important to remain flexible. Far too many hunters fall into the rut of relying completely on a single system for success during the entire season. Such an approach is going to do nothing but get you into trouble. As I've pointed out, even though it's hard to ignore the effectiveness of such a practice, sitting in a tree stand isn't *always* the best plan of attack.

There are any number of factors that can alter the normal movement patterns and change the behavior of whitetail bucks. As most experienced deer hunters know, it's times like these that might warrant the use of an alternate tactic.

To attain and then stay at a high level of success, trophy whitetail hunters must be adept at reading and understanding current situations. Then, to successfully deal with those situations, they must be experts at coming up with tactics that will prove effective. Certainly, sneaking and peeking is one such tactic.

Greg's Proven Pointers

- I first started using the sneak-and-peek tactic because it offered me a respite from sitting on a tree stand. But my main reason using the tactic now is because it has proven so darn effective.

- Although sneaking and peeking can be effective in almost any type of terrain, it's most effective in hill/ridge country. Regardless of the terrain, you must always make sure that wind conditions are favorable for a sneak and peek hunt.

- Sneaking and peeking allows you to effectively traverse a lot of ground in a relatively short amount of time.

- Binoculars are a must for sneaking and peeking. You don't want to be using your rifle scope to check out potential targets.

CHAPTER FOURTEEN

When Bucks Disappear

Considering the whitetail's current popularity, the opening of gun-deer season is one of the biggest annual events in many parts of the country. I would venture to say that the vast majority of deer hunters head into the woods on opening morning fully expecting that, by day's end, their tag will be firmly affixed to a trophy buck.

Unfortunately, reality dictates that only a very small percentage of opening-day hunters will actually realize their dream. The rest will head home with unfilled tags and considerably less confidence. Still, most of these people will retain just enough hope to make a concerted effort on day two. But what happens when legal shooting time expires on the second day and their tags are still in their pockets?

Believe it or not, I've actually seen some deer hunters pack their bags at the end of opening weekend and head for home. As far as they're concerned, the season is over. After all, everybody knows that trying to find a big buck after the first two days is like looking for the proverbial needle in the haystack.

It's true. Mature bucks seem to possess the uncanny ability to literally fall off the face of the earth after opening weekend. Even with a fresh tracking snow, I've often found that it's darn near impossible at this time of the season to find even one set of huge, hoof-dragging deer tracks coursing through the woods.

Finding less and less sign as the season progresses can be downright exasperating for the average deer hunter. From personal experience, I can tell you that it's a pretty helpless feeling when you know one of your favorite hunting areas has been "burned out." Believe me, this sort of thing happened a lot during my early years as a deer hunter.

The most frustrating part of all this was that I knew for certain that it was possible to kill big bucks later in the season. Several very experienced hunters in my area were doing this very thing! In fact, one local hunter had made a habit of bringing in better-than-average bucks late in the season. It was after I'd admired yet another of this guy's trophies that I made a silent vow to become just as proficient as him.

Where Bucks Go to Avoid Humans

Fortunately, I was able to garner a bit of very valuable information from this successful mid-season hunter. Still, the guy could tell me only so much. A lot of what I've since learned came about only after I adopted a very strict work ethic. Simply put, I spent every free minute attempting to figure out how the big bucks in my hunting areas were evading me.

One thing quickly became apparent. The amount of human intrusion into a specific area played a *huge* role in how the bucks in that area would behave. Of greater interest than this, however, were the kinds of places bigger bucks would seek out in their attempts to avoid contact with humans. To help illustrate just what lengths mature bucks will go in their attempts to stay alive, I'd like to relate a story I heard some years back.

A huge 10-point buck had been seen crossing a main highway just before light every morning. After crossing the road, the buck would walk through the neatly trimmed lawn near a small house. He would stop at the back of the lawn, on the edge of a small, very thick patch of brush. Before stepping into the cover, the buck would check his surroundings one last time. Satisfied that he hadn't been followed to his personal little sanctuary, the old buck would then enter the tangle of briars and popple brush and lay down.

Although the 10-pointer wasn't aware of it, his retreat into the bedding area was witnessed many times. An old man who lived in the small house with the neatly trimmed lawn studied the big buck's routine almost daily. The man had absolutely no interest in killing the big deer. And even if he did, the act would have been illegal. You see, the old man's house and property laid well within the city limits of a small town. So he has been a mere spectator—but a spectator who found himself amazed at the cunning and guile displayed by a true survivor.

Of course, a small bit of the above story is based on speculation, but the rest is based on fact. The big buck in the story, which was eventually found dead by a good friend of mine, *did* spend a good deal of his time within the city limits of a small town. And an old man *did* watch the deer wander near his house during the pre-dawn light on many occasions. It's no wonder the buck lived long enough to grow a set of antlers that, at the time of his death, grossed in the low 190s as a typical.

Do you think the survival pattern displayed by this monster buck is one very rarely duplicated? Well, the fact that he spent a most of the daylight hours bedded within the city limits may be unusual, but the fact that he did something unique in his attempt to stay alive shouldn't come as a surprise—at least not to most seri-

Mature bucks are masters of the evasion game. Deer of this caliber possess the uncanny ability to "drop off the face of the earth" whenever they desire.

A lot of hunters would be surprised if they knew about some of the things mature bucks do to survive. These same people would also be surprised to learn just how little cover it takes to hide a monster buck.

ous deer hunters. (I have to wonder how many hunters continually found mega-buck sign in the area, yet were unable to figure out where the buck responsible for that sign was hiding out.)

Big bucks have a very irritating way of dropping out of sight during gun-deer seasons. I'm under the impression that most big deer actually get into some type of survival patterns long before opening day of gun season. A number of things can and often do happen to clue the deer herd that it might be wise to change its ways.

For example, my home state's small game season begins the week before our archery season for deer. While not numerous, there are just enough squirrel, rabbit and grouse hunters walking around in the woods to put big bucks on alert. And once a big buck is on alert, his demeanor changes drastically.

The Wisdom of Age

The most effective weapon a mature whitetail can use against us is to adopt a strict nocturnal movement pattern. Almost as effective, however, is finding a place or places where human intrusion is nearly nil. Believe me, if there are any hiding places within the range of a whitetail buck that offer him three essential ingredients—adequate cover, quick access to food and safe escape routes—the buck will know of them.

Regardless of the area, there are always going to be a certain number of bucks that will survive long enough to reach their full trophy potential.

From what I've seen, however, there still are quite a few hunters who have trouble identifying such spots. I believe this is because these hunters still haven't grasped just how different mature bucks are from rest of the deer herd. If you remember one thing from this chapter, let it be this: The habits, travel patterns and general behavior traits of younger bucks *seldom* resemble those displayed by older age-class bucks.

I feel strongly that this is the main reason a lot of deer hunters can't establish any sort of consistent success on mature bucks later in the season. They simply don't understand the vast behavioral differences that exist between immature and mature animals. Consequently, these individuals end up spending most of their time hunting in spots where they stand virtually no chance of killing a big buck.

I think it's important to point out that no matter where whitetails are found there is a certain percentage of the buck herd that will reach an age that allows them to attain their maximum trophy potential. Trust me, even in areas that see a very heavy concentration of hunters and an extremely large annual deer kill, there are always a few bucks that live long enough to reach maturity. Somehow, this select handful of bucks finds a way to evade the hordes of hunters that head afield every year.

What is that small minority of the buck herd doing to ensure their survival from one year to the next? The most obvious answer is that these bucks are finding select spots that hunters are either overlooking or simply avoiding. Interestingly, there may be some cases when this perfect hideout will encompass many acres. But I've also seen cases where the "perfect" buck sanctuary consisted of less than an acre of cover.

In farmland or open country, whitetail bucks that are able to stay alive long enough to reach maturity could be labeled masters of evasion. In this sort of terrain, I'm of the belief that any piece of cover big enough to hold a rooster pheasant can also hide a big whitetail buck. A patch of grass or brush, no matter what the size, could be big enough to adequately hide the buck of your dreams. A friend of mine recently told me of an experience he had that illustrates this perfectly.

It was the mid-point of Wisconsin's nine-day gun season for deer. My friend was driving down a back-country road, trying to decide where he was going to hunt later in the day. As he was driving and thinking, he happened to look out into a large alfalfa field. About 100 yards from the road lay a small, two-acre patch consisting of tall swamp grass and scattered clumps of tag alder.

My friend immediately pulled over to the side of the road and spent a few seconds looking at the tiny patch of cover. Then he grabbed his rifle and headed across the alfalfa field. "I hadn't taken ten steps into that patch of cover when a huge buck jumped up out of its bed and went crashing off," he told me. "I was both surprised and more than a little excited. As a result, I shot way too fast." Just that quickly, the buck was over a nearby hill and gone."

Once he realized the buck was indeed gone, my friend did a little investigating. Not only did he find the buck's bed from that day, he also found beds from the preceeding five or six days. Interestingly, all the beds were in a radius of less than ten yards.

"I figured that since I'd shot at the buck, there was no way he'd come back and lay in that patch of cover again," my friend told me. "But I just had to check it out anyway. So the next day I went back with a couple of hunting partners. Unbelievably, the buck was bedded in the almost the exact same spot. Due to some terrible shooting, however, he managed to escape once more."

My friend and his two partners returned to the tiny patch of cover the very next day. "We were more convinced than ever that the buck wouldn't be laying in the grass again," he stated. "But just to be safe, I decided to sneak around and take up a position over the hill where the buck had run the first two times. My two buddies were still fifty-yards from the cover when the buck jumped and ran. Lucky for me, he followed the exact route he'd taken the two previous days. I dropped him with one shot."

Whether you're talking big woods or farmland, the basic philosophy remains constant: Mature bucks make it a point to seek out those pieces of cover that ensure they won't be bothered by hunters.

I'm sure some hunters find it hard to believe that the buck returned to the grass after being shot at on two different occasions. But I've heard countless stories of hunters running big bucks out of the same pockets of cover almost on a daily basis. Maybe the fact that the deer continues to escape strengthens his confidence in his current sanctuary.

What Makes a Good Hiding Spot?

Brushy fencelines, a small patch of weeds or an overlooked woodlot all are places that a big buck could use as a hideout. As I've learned, *any* patch of cover that seems out of the way or too obvious to hide a deer, might be doing just that. It's for these exact reasons that a buck will take up residence in such places. He can usually remain undisturbed and, above all, safe for the duration of the season. Remember, when it comes to surviving, big deer don't consider any patch of cover as being too obvious or too far out of the way.

Another excellent place to look for spooked bucks in farmland country is set-aside or government CRP land. These are parcels for which the government has paid a landowner not to put into crops. After just one year of dormancy, the resulting weed crop is tall enough to hide the biggest bucks. Again, these fields might be anywhere from five acres to one hundred acres (or more) in size. But size doesn't seem to play as large a role in a buck's decision on where to hide as the contributing factors mentioned earlier—hunting pressure, quick access to food, adequate cover and safe escape routes.

When looking for sanctuary from hunters, big woods bucks will seek the same types of cover as their farmland cousins. Unlike farm country deer, however, big woods whitetails almost always have more options from which to choose. There are two reasons for this. First, hunting pressure is usually not as intense in big woods environments. And second, big woods deer have a lot more cover at their disposal. These two reasons can make finding and then killing big woods bucks a slightly more difficult task later in the season, but rest assured, it can be done.

Although it may seem as if every available piece of cover is being hounded, in big woods that's very rarely the case. Almost without exception, there will be pockets of cover that are experiencing little or no hunting pressure. But to find these pockets, you must first get to know the lay of the land. Taking the time to walk and familiarize yourself with country in and around your hunting areas, either in the spring or before the season opens, can go a long way in determining the final outcome of your mid-season hunts.

I like to concentrate my attention on swampy areas, briar thickets, 2- to 10-year-old clearcuts and areas where a good number of trees have been blown down. I'll also check out places where visibility is extremely limited. The later in the season it gets, the more a big whitetail will prefer to take up residence in such locations.

Another key to finding disappearing bucks is paying attention to what other hunters are doing. One of the main reasons my big woods success rate is so impressive is because I've learned how to quickly and accurately pattern other hunters. The beauty of this is that I'm able to identify if a certain place is being neglected or avoided. And trust me, it makes no difference if the spot is one mile or 100 yards from the nearest road. If it offers a buck all the ingredients he needs for survival, there most likely will be a big buck hiding in the spot.

For many years, I was under the impression that the farther off the road I hunted, the bigger the bucks I'd find. But while this may be true in some cases, it certainly isn't true all the time. I can think of three good bucks I've taken while sitting within 300 yards of a major highway. These deer were living closer to the roads because hunting pressure "way back in" had become very intense.

Small, well-organized pushes can be an effective way of dealing with disappearing bucks. Before making these pushes, however, you must ensure that everyone involved understands the importance of walking every square foot of each piece of cover—regardless of the size. I can't stress enough how little cover it takes to completely hide a huge buck.

Once while pheasant hunting, my dog jumped a beautiful 10-point buck and two does out of a tiny patch of knee high grass. The amazing thing is that I had just stomped through that grass myself. Those three deer had remained hidden, even though I had walked within a few yards of them. You never stop learning things in this sport.

I've enjoyed quite a bit of mid-season success while occupying stands that were situated on the edge of a chunk of prime buck-hiding cover. Of course, it's going to

Big bucks occasionally slip out of their bedding areas for a midday snack. In most cases, these feedings take place in isolated areas, where hunting pressure is light or nonexistent.

take a bit of scouting to determine where such pockets of cover are located. You must then establish stand sites that allow you to effectively hunt the cover.

There's something else you must keep in mind. Mature bucks are tough customers. However, they really become a special case once they've been harassed and shot at. Remember, whitetails that are in a strict survival mode are going to be ultra-sensitive and highly reclusive. Obviously, it's imperative you keep a very low profile when hunting on the edge of prime looking cover.

It almost goes without saying that wind direction should be uppermost in your mind. Sitting on a stand just one time when the wind is wrong could ruin your chances for the rest of the season. Also, make sure you establish walking routes that let you slip into and out of your stand areas without causing a disturbance.

Do What Other Hunters *Aren't* Doing

There's another relatively simple tactic that can work extremely well for dealing with spooked bucks: Staying in the woods when everyone else is heading out. Big bucks can become very proficient at timing the height of human activity in the woods. It doesn't take them long to realize they're almost as safe moving around at high noon as they are at midnight. Consequently, they learn to adjust their travel times accordingly. On occasion, try staying in the woods and skipping your own noon feeding.

Two very fine whitetail bucks were taken close to my home during a recent season. Cleo Hoel of Eau Claire, Wisconsin, took a big, 160-class 10-pointer while hunting on a tract of land that borders a prime big buck hiding area. Just before legal shooting time expired on the second day of the season, the buck left the safety of his sanctuary and headed for a nearby alfalfa field. Cleo just happened to be in the right place and at the right time.

Less than 20 miles away, Leo Zeman of rural Bloomer shot a huge 12 pointer that grossed more than 170 typical points. Leo's strategy was far from complicated or difficult. Basically, he stayed on his stand after a lot of other hunters had already walked out of the surrounding woods. It was 10:30 a.m. when the trophy deer followed a doe out into an open field. Leo's .30-.30 put the buck down for keeps.

Many times, towards the end of our deer season, I've heard hunters claim that "there aren't any big bucks left in the area." This train of thought, although far from accurate, is completely understandable. The truth is that many of those hunters don't know their hunting areas well enough to figure out where the deer will be hiding *after* opening day.

I've always found it especially intriguing that trophy-size whitetails can continue to exist in areas that experience extremely heavy hunting pressure. Just this past year, and within five miles of my home, I picked up a shed antler from a very mature buck. Interestingly, the deer lives in the heart of an area that undergoes intense pressure during our gun season. Still, the buck has managed to come up with a very dependable system for staying alive from one year to the next.

Undoubtedly, this system entails taking up residence in a quality hiding spot *before* deer season opens. He then stays in this hiding spot—at least during daylight hours—until after the season has closed. Unless someone who hunts that area suddenly becomes adept at hunting disappearing bucks in the near future, I'm convinced the old monarch will die of natural causes. And rightfully so.

Greg's Proven Pointers

- The key to figuring out how big bucks can "disappear" is to first accept the fact that mature whitetail bucks simply don't act in a "normal" manner.

- Pressure from other humans, which includes deer hunters and small game hunters, often has a lot to do with why deer suddenly disappear.

- Big bucks don't need a lot of cover to disappear. My philosophy is that if a patch of cover is big enough to hide a rooster pheasant, it can also hide a big buck.

- Don't get into the rut of thinking that early morning/late afternoon are the only times worth hunting. Provided certain conditions are right, hunting during the middle of the day can be just as productive as the aforementioned times.

CHAPTER FIFTEEN

Finding and Hunting Hidden Edges

I'm sure most experienced deer hunters have heard that white-tailed deer are edge creatures. Take my word for it, no more accurate description of the species exists. All deer, from the smallest fawns to the largest bucks, relate to edges.

Unfortunately, I believe a constant touting of the "edge creature" factor has given many deer hunters the wrong impression. Much of the confusion has been caused by individual interpretation of the term "edge." From what I've been able to gather, some hunters are under the impression that edges exist only where an expanse of open ground (a field) butts up to a chunk of cover (a woods). Nothing could be further from the truth.

Regardless of the habitat, there are a number of different types of edges that usually exist within the bounds of available whitetail cover. And depending upon the big variable—hunting pressure—whitetails normally relate to all these different types of edges. What's more, some of these edges are "hidden." This makes them prime places for big bucks to establish often-visited rub- and scrape-lines. Even more interesting is the fact that mature bucks often visit these hidden-edge signposts during daylight hours.

Now, this isn't to say that mature whitetail bucks don't relate to more obvious, open edges. They certainly spend a great amount of time rubbing, scraping and traveling in such locations. But as most hunters will attest, until the very late stages of the pre-rut, the majority of this activity occurs under the cover of darkness.

So when I speak of hunting along edges, I'm usually not referring to open field edges. Rather, my edge-hunting philosophy generally centers around hidden edges—in other words, those that are found inside the available whitetail cover.

This is what a ot of hunters think of when they hear the work edge: A place where an expense of open ground butts up to a chunk of cover.

There are many different types of these "inside edges." But although each may have a slightly different appearance or occur in slightly different habitat, they all have one thing in common: If there are big whitetail bucks in the vicinity, they will most likely be relating to these edges.

It's my intent in this chapter to make hunters aware of some of the different types of edges that could exist in their deer hunting areas. I'll also discuss the most effective strategies for locating and hunting along different edges. Hopefully, the following information will help you pinpoint some of these big buck hot spots in your neck of the woods.

Cover Edges

Cover edges are the most common types of edges—and some of the easiest to locate. Most cover edges occur when an expanse of rather open forest butts up to a much thicker piece of cover. It's there, right on the edge of the transition from open to thick forest, where one normally finds the majority of big buck sign.

A bit of common sense can tell you why whitetails, especially mature bucks, prefer to travel along the edges of the thicker cover. By doing so, they're able to visibly check the more open terrain, both for danger and the presence of other deer, while at the same time never being more than a single jump away from the safety and security offered by the thick cover.

Hunting Inside Edges

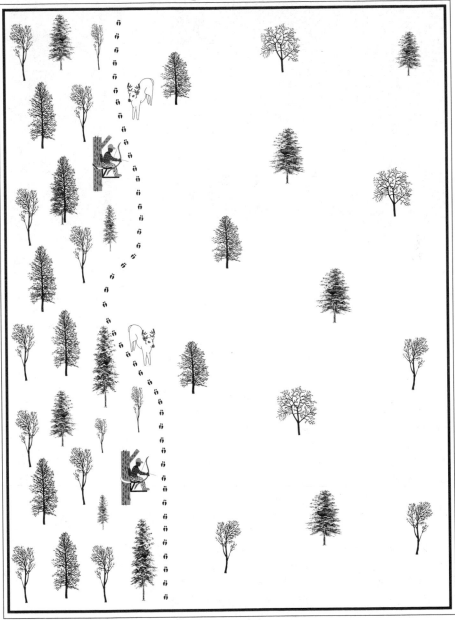

I've had a tremendous amount of big buck success while hunting along inside edges. Basically, these kind of edges occur where a rather open expanse of forest butts up to a much thicker chunk of cover, like a swamp or regrowth area.

Potential Stand Sites

Buck Travel Routes (Rub/Scrape-Lines)

I spend a lot of time sitting on stand sites located along the edges of swamps and regrowth areas. These types of hidden edges have been very productive for me.

Although there are many different types of cover edges, I prefer to concentrate my hunting efforts along those edges that border swamps and re-growth areas. Along with traveling the edges of such places, big bucks also will establish a number of different corridors that lead them directly into and out of the thicker cover.

Usually, I'm able to pinpoint the most often used exit/entry routes simply by walking the runway that parallels the cover. I'll check every runway that peels off the parallel runway and heads into the thicker cover. What I'm looking for is rub and scrape sign. By keeping a mental record of which runway(s) show the most buck sign, I'll be able to make a fairly easy decision as to where my stand(s) should be placed.

One of my early big buck bow-kills came along an inside edge. My portable stand had been positioned in a large birch tree, roughly 25 yards from the edge of a huge tamarack swamp. By the way, it hadn't taken hours of scouting to decide were to place my stand either; the final decision turned out to be a virtual no-brainer.

You see, just a small bit of scouting had led me to discover a very obvious and fresh rub-line exiting the swamp. That rub-line then continued along the edge of the swamp and right past my stand position. Since the whitetails in that part of the country were in the final stages of their pre-rut rituals, I figured this was *the* best place to ambush a mature animal. My decision proved to be right on the money.

The buck showed up an hour before dark on the very first afternoon I sat in the edge stand. The 10-pointer was well out of bow range and moving in super-slow motion when I first saw him. Still, there was no doubt in my mind that, eventually, he would end up within spitting distance of my tree stand. All I had to do was display the patience and restraint so crucial in such situations—and to make an accurate shot when the time came.

After thoroughly thrashing a clump of tag alder, the buck resumed his original course of travel. The big deer weaved his way through the thick cover along the swamp edge, grunting with every step he took. At 30 yards, he stopped, looked in my direction, and then came walking out of the swamp, straight toward the tree in which I was perched.

When he was a mere 15 yards away and directly head-on, the buck stopped once more and scrutinized the forest floor directly under my stand site. My heart stayed in my throat the entire time. After nearly a minute of this, the buck convinced himself that nothing was out of the ordinary. Then he turned and walked straight away from me.

I knew what the deer had in mind, so while his rump was still toward me, I came to full draw. As expected, he got to the runway that ran along the edge of the swamp and turned broadside. I quickly estimated the range to be a shade over 20 yards. The sight pin floated around a bit, then locked in on the crease just behind the buck's front shoulder. When he stretched that leg to take a step, I touched my release. Even before the arrow reached him, I knew the 10-pointer was mine. Indeed, he made it only 40 yards before succumbing to the double-lung hit.

Several years have passed since that successful hunt took place. However, since that time, I've exploited the exact tactic I used on that day to harvest several more bucks as they traveled along inside edges.

Water Edges

Water plays a larger role in creating an edge situation than any other natural factor. And it makes no difference if that water is in the form of a creek, river, beaver pond or lake. If the water is located in an area frequented by whitetails, those deer will be using the edges of the natural barrier. A few years back, while doing some post-season scouting in the big woods of northern Wisconsin, I happened to discover a small pond. There was so much rub and scrape sign along one edge of that pond that it bordered on being unbelievable. At first, I couldn't figure out why the bucks had concentrated so much of their activity along that one particular edge. But a bit of looking around showed me the exact reason.

A short distance through the woods, perhaps 100 yards from that particular edge of the pond, I found a large stand of mature red oak trees. There had been an exceptionally heavy acorn crop that year, which meant the spot was serving as a prime food source for all the whitetails in the vicinity.

When coming to feed, it was apparent the bucks would approach from the downwind side of the oaks. Interestingly, this put them along the edge of the pond. Obviously, those deer had figured out that by walking along the pond, they were assured no danger could approach from the water side. They then trusted their noses to warn them of any lurking danger from the direction of the oaks. What a sense of security!

Edges created by the presence of water—whether it's a lake, pond, river or creek—are always good places to check for signs of buck activity. Remember, whitetails relate quite strongly to drainages!

You can expect to find the same sort of concentrated buck activity along creeks and rivers. Usually, the vegetation found along any waterway is quite thick, so it provides more-than-adequate cover. In addition, much of that same cover also serves as preferred browse-type food for whitetails—in effect, it does double duty for the deer.

I should mention that I've often run into a problem when attempting to find quality stand sites along water edges. In most cases, I've found that the deer had established their travel routes very close to the edge of the water. Worse, they usually only travel along these routes when the wind is blowing from the cover and out toward the water.

Of course, this means that if you want to escape detection, you have to place your stands on the side of the runway closest to the water. But as I've so painfully found out, there isn't always a tree suitable for my stand in these places. And in some instances when I have found a tree, there wasn't a whole lot of background cover available. Unless you're extremely careful in such situations, it's relatively easy to get "skylined" by the deer.

Topography Edges

Topography edges are caused by a sudden or drastic change in the natural lay of the land. For the most part, these changes occur in mountainous, ridge, bluff and hill country.

A perfect example of the types of edges I'm talking about can be found in an area located in the southwestern part of my home state of Wisconsin. Here, the majority of the terrain is comprised of wooded bluffs. These bluffs are extremely steep and rugged, which makes hunting in that area a tough challenge. Not only does the topography work against bow-hunters, but constantly swirling winds often ruin the most perfect set-ups.

Because of the swirling winds, much of the energy expended by deer hunters in this area is spent seeking out stand sites that will provide them with true winds. Anyone who is even remotely familiar with hunting hilly terrain knows this means most of your set-ups are going to be located either at the very bottoms or very tops of the hills.

Interestingly, rather expansive flats are situated on top of many of the bluffs. As you might suspect, the whitetails living in the area relate strongly to the flats. Along with being used as regular travel corridors, the flats also play host to a great deal of pre-rut and rut activity.

But, the whitetails that reside here don't walk just anywhere when traversing these flats. In fact, they usually restrict their travels to a couple of key spots on the flats. True to form, these spots allow them to exploit the terrain fully to their advantage.

My friend Tom Indrebo has been chasing trophy whitetails in the rugged bluff country for years. Along with trying to fill his own tag each year, Tom also brings in a number of clients for his trophy whitetail outfitting business.

Tom explained to me that one of the best ways to kill a big buck in the bluff country is by setting up along the natural edges found on the flats. "There are a couple key places to look for such edges on the flats," he told me. "Of course, one such place is along cover edges. But the other, equally productive spot, is along the edge of the flat, right where it drops off into the deep valleys."

I've spent quite a bit of time hunting in this rugged bluff country. As a result, I'm fully aware of exactly why the deer love running the edges of those break lines. By doing so, they're able to use their visual abilities to not only scan the flat, but also to look deep down into the wooded valleys. They do this in an attempt to locate other deer *and* to check for threats to their well-being. Again, it's purely a matter of the deer exploiting the terrain in a specific area to their advantage.

One more thing—the flats I've described are not found solely in areas where the terrain is very steep and/or rugged. These types of flats can exist even in slightly rolling terrain. The whitetails that live in such terrain will relate quite strongly to the flats. Further, the majority of deer activity will be concentrated along the outside edges of the flats. Even though the flat might be only slightly higher than the surrounding terrain, it does increase the deer's line of sight. Again, this gives them a slight advantage when checking for danger and other deer.

Food Source Edges

Flats warrant your attention for another reason. Years ago, the farmers in the area realized that clearing some of these flats would dramatically increase their tillable acreage. So every year, you can count on a crop of either corn, alfalfa or soybeans on the flats. As any experienced deer hunter knows, all of the afore-mentioned foods are highly delectable to whitetails. I'm sure you can imagine the drawing ability of the hidden food sources.

When it comes to hunting mature whitetails, I'm not a big fan of setting up along field edges. However, as with any other situation, there are exceptions to the rule. This is certainly one of those exceptions.

Actually, it doesn't really matter if you're hunting hilly terrain, flatlands or something in between. Anytime you have a situation where a crop attractant is completely surrounded by cover, it's bound to be a hot spot. The only factor that can negate the drawing ability of such a food source is extremely heavy hunting pressure.

But the outside perimeter of hidden crop attractants aren't the only places where hunters can expect to see some edge activity. There also are many in-woods food sources where edge situations exist. Stands of oak and areas that have recently been logged or burned (stimulating desired re-growth) are just a couple of examples. The edges of old homesteaded fields are another excellent place to check for signs of feeding activity. Of course, there may be other hidden food sources you're aware of that are found only in your part of the country.

Fence Line Edges

The first thing that's bound to come to mind when mentioning fence lines is the fact that they're found out in the open, on the edges of fields. But again, I'm

Any crop attractant that's completely surrounded by woods has the potential to be a big buck hot spot. This is especially true if hunting pressure is relatively light.

talking here about hidden fence lines. There are some great hunting opportunities to be found near such edge situations.

It's a given that whitetails love to follow fence lines. So it only stands to reason that anytime they're able to follow such an arterial, while at the same time remaining hidden, they'll take advantage of the situation. While I've seen many examples of this scenario, one in particular stands out in my mind

I had hunted a certain woodlot for several years, and it had proven to be a virtual buck hot spot. But then during the off-season one year, something happened that appeared might put a kink in my game plan. The farmer who owned the land decided to use part of the woodlot as a pasture for his beef cattle. Unfortunately, that portion of the woodlot he had decided to pasture was where I had seen the majority of buck movement over the years.

At first I viewed the introduction of the cattle as a hindrance and a real threat to my chances for success. However, it took only a couple of trips into the area to show me that, if anything, the presence of the bovines was a great asset. Before the cattle came onto the scene, there were a number of different travel options available to the deer. Once the cattle were turned loose, however, the whitetails abandoned their travel routes through that part of the woods. (In my part of the country, cattle and deer simply don't cohabitate.)

While doing some in-season scouting I found that the deer were now restricting their travels to one spot in particular. And that spot was right along the new fence line that bordered one side of the pastured area. On the first afternoon I sat on

181

a stand overlooking the fence line, I had five different bucks walk by within bow range. Repeated hunts to the spot also paid off with sightings of antlered animals.

I should point out that the presence of cattle isn't a requirement for fence lines to be "hot" travel routes. Whitetails just love to establish travel routes along fence lines. In fact, I've found that mature bucks often establish travel routes along fence lines that course through rather open woodlots.

Double Edges

My brother Jeff arrowed a fine 140-class whitetail during a recent season. That buck was taken as a result of my brother exploiting a rare but highly productive double-edge situation. Jeff's tree stand was placed so he could overlook an in-woods fence line that coursed along a cover edge—where thick cover transitioned into more open woods. The heavy-horned 8-pointer walked by at 20 yards on the very first afternoon Jeff sat on his newly placed stand.

I've also taken advantage of some double-edge situations. The most recent case that comes to mind occurred during the 1995 archery season. The first time I sat on the stand provided me with absolute proof that I had set up in the perfect spot. On that afternoon, I managed to rattle in a tremendous buck. The sure Boone & Crockett contender walked to within 30 yards of my stand site. Unfortunately, my normally dependable eyes told my brain the range was more like 20 yards. As a result, I used the wrong sight pin. My arrow skimmed just under the chest of the huge 6x6 typical.

But my bout of bad luck didn't last very long. The next time I sat on the stand a 130-class 10-pointer made the mistake of walking by within bow range. The razor-sharp broadhead did its job, and the buck left a profuse blood-trail all the way to his final resting place.

What sort of a double-edge situation was I exploiting on this hunt? My stand was located on the edge of a huge CRP field, but instead of setting up just anywhere, I had elected to put the stand in an obvious corner. At this point, a rather wide, brush-covered fence line bumped up against a woods. The woods then jutted out into the CRP field perhaps 50 yards.

Some people might consider this more of a double-corner situation. And I would normally agree—had my stand been placed *inside the woods*. However, my stand was situated along the edge of the CRP field, where the *edge* of the woods and the *edge* of the brushy fence line came together. A double-edge!

Still, there are cases where double edges might be found inside the woods. For instance, I know of places where there are narrow strips of open timber that are bordered on both sides by much thicker woods. In most cases, I've found an abundance of buck sign along each edge. Interestingly, some of these strips of open timber are narrow enough that I'm able to cover either edge merely by placing my tree stand in the middle of the strip.

The great thing about edge hunting is that it can be used in conjunction with any method of hunting for trophy whitetails. Waiting in ambush along known buck travel corridors, standing watch over steaming scrapes or posting along

Hunting Double Edges

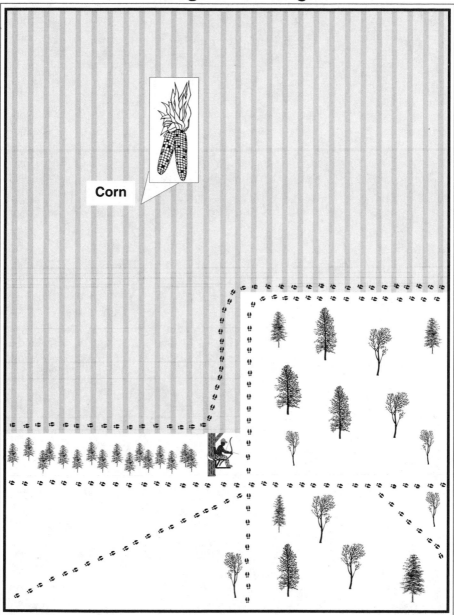

Corn

In my opinion, this is a perfect example of a double edge. In most situations, whitetails will follow the edges created by the brush line and the woods. By the way, double edges are also great places from which to try and call in a big buck.

Potential Stand Sites

Buck Travel Routes (Rub/Scrape-Lines)

I shot this buck along a rare, double-edge situation. Whitetail bucks generally do a good deal of scraping, rubbing and traveling along these unique corridors.

active rub-lines are all effective tactics. But they become even more productive if your set-ups are used in conjunction with some sort of hidden edge.

Setting up along hidden edges also can be a highly effective tactic for those deer hunters who prefer to incorporate calling in their hunting efforts. Believe me, giving big bucks the option of approaching along the edge of thick cover can do nothing but increase your response rate. The only prerequisites are making sure your stands are placed within bow range of the edge and *always* using the wind to your advantage.

As with any tactic specifically designed to get you within range of trophy whitetails, hunting along hidden edges does not guarantee a big buck every time out. However, if used properly, this strategy should help increase your success rate. The realists involved in this sport know that's the most we can expect.

Greg's Proven Pointers

- Whitetails are edge creatures—but edges exist in more places than you might think.

- My favorite types of edges to hunt are those created by a swamp or thick re-growth area. These places are almost always HOT!

- Whitetails have a natural affinity for water, and more specifically drainages. Don't overlook the natural edge situation created by lakes, ponds, rivers and creeks.

- Some crop attractant edges can be productive, even for mature bucks. This is expecially true when the crop attractant is nearly surrounded by thick cover.

- There might be other types of edges aside from the ones I've highlighted in this chapter. The key is to pay attention to how the deer in your specific hunting areas relate to their surroundings.

CHAPTER SIXTEEN

Hunting Hill-Country Deer

I've heard (and been involved in) more than my share of arguments regarding what sort of terrain is the toughest of all in which to hunt for big bucks. After paying close attention to these arguments, and after spending a great deal of time hunting in varying terrain, I've come to the conclusion that hill-country whitetails rank near the top of the "most-challenging" list.

"There just ain't no way to effectively hunt that kind of terrain," a fellow hunter told me recently. "It seems no matter where I set up the wind is constantly swirling. Most times, the deer end up picking me off long before they get close enough for a bow shot. I'm about ready to give up and try hunting some flat country!"

I'm not going to argue that hunting for hill-country deer isn't a tough deal. And I do agree with the aforementioned hunter that swirling winds are a *very* real problem in hilly terrain. However, I'm of the opinion that, just like any situation that initially appears impossible, there are solutions to the problems facing those who hunt whitetail bucks in hill country.

In this chapter I'm going to cover the intimate details involved in becoming an effective hill-country deer hunter. Hopefully, I'll give hunters some insight into figuring out where their stands should be placed. I'll also discuss how time of year can have a bearing on stand-placement.

But before going any further, I'd like to clear up one matter. I don't want readers misled by the term "hill country." This term is meant to include bluffs, ridges, mountains or whatever type of "hill country" you might be hunting.

Hill-country whitetails are a tough target indeed. But there are some strategies that prove consistently effective on big bucks that reside in this type of terrain.

Following the Path of Least Resistance

One of the most important things that hill-country deer hunters must realize is that, when it comes deciding where they're going to walk, whitetails are a lot like humans. Just like us, deer prefer to move about their ranges via routes that allow them to expend the least amount of energy. And whenever possible, whitetails also like to have a bit of cover to go along with this easy access.

With this in mind, it becomes easier to determine where the deer are going to establish their primary travel routes. For instance, if you've ever watched hill-country whitetails move about their range, you'll notice they very seldom walk along the side of a hill. This is especially true if the hill is quite steep.

Actually, four-legged animals in general aren't all that fond of traveling along sidehills (but then neither are two-legged animals). This is another valuable bit of information, because *in most cases*, you can forget about establishing stand-sites on the side of a hill. Now, you'll notice I said in *most* cases.

Just like with other aspects of hunting for whitetails, there are exceptions to the rule. Whitetails very seldom travel very far along the side of a hill. But I will admit that deer and other animals will occasionally break this rule. And in every instance where I've seen this to be the case, there was a situation that made "side-hilling" a practical solution.

Even on the steepest of hills, you'll occasionally find a slight shelf than runs along the side of that hill. In some instances, these shelves will run for quite some

Hunting Hillside Shelves

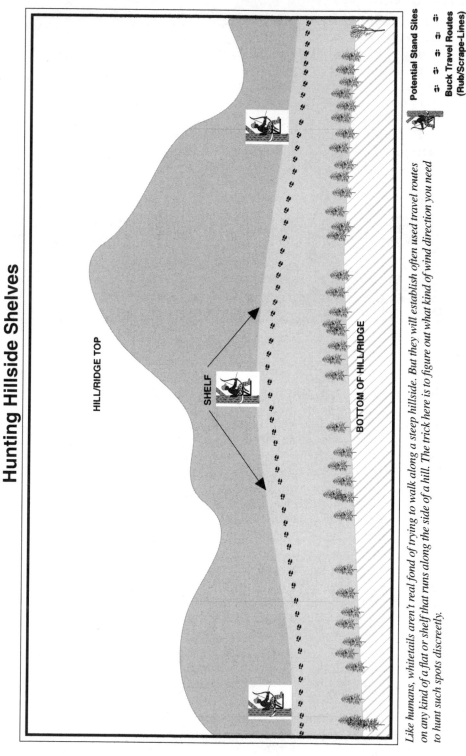

HILL/RIDGE TOP

SHELF

BOTTOM OF HILL/RIDGE

Potential Stand Sites

Buck Travel Routes
(Rub/Scrape-Lines)

Like humans, whitetails aren't real fond of trying to walk along a steep hillside. But they will establish often used travel routes on any kind of a flat or shelf that runs along the side of a hill. The trick here is to figure out what kind of wind direction you need to hunt such spots discreetly.

distance. And if they do, you can bet the local whitetail herd will establish a primary travel route that follows that table or shelf for as far as it goes.

Big whitetail bucks have a real affinity for traveling along these shelves—and I think I know why. As I've pointed out repeatedly (contrary to what some hunters believe) whitetail deer *do* rely heavily on their sense of sight. In fact, whenever possible, big bucks establish travel routes that allow them to use their eyes as much as any of their other senses.

First and foremost, they are going to use their eyesight to help them detect threats to their well-being. Whitetails seem to have caught on to the fact that most predators, including man, concentrate their hunting efforts on the tops and/or the bottoms of hills. By walking along these shelves, bucks can visually check for danger both on the ridge tops and in the woods below.

As we all know, visibility in the woods increases dramatically once the leaves fall. (This yearly occurrence just happens to take place right before the breeding period.) I've seen many cases where rutting bucks, in their search for hot does, walk along hillside shelves and use their eyes to check for signs of antlerless deer activity in the wooded valleys and crop lands below.

Blowin' in the Wind

There's a good chance that any table or shelf you find in hill country will be a preferred travel route of the resident buck herd. However, hunters must be aware of one very important bit of information before setting up in such spots: This is a place where you're going to be susceptible to swirling wind conditions.

Because you're hunting on a sidehill, any wind that blows directly at the side of that hill is going to wind up swirling up and around you. Believe me, it's going to be extremely difficult to get a big buck within bow range of your stand under such conditions.

Your best bet for hunting shelves is to wait for a wind that is blowing parallel to the hillside where you plan to set-up. You can also escape detection by hunting when the wind is blowing into the opposite side of the hill. (Which means you'll be in a relatively wind-free spot.) In either case, provided wind velocity remains steady and the direction true, you shouldn't have a problem with swirling winds.

I remember how swirling winds once ruined what seemed to be a foolproof plan. For nearly a month prior to opening day of our archery season, I had been watching the same little cavalcade of bucks come to a lush alfalfa field. As you might imagine, my observations had taught me much about each of those six bucks, including their individual habits and, more importantly, their movement patterns. If ever I had seen something that appeared on the surface to be a sure-thing, this was it.

From all appearances, the plan I had formulated seemed fool-proof. I was going to wait until mid-morning on opening day, walk into the woods and put my portable treestand in place. Then I was going to return to hunt from the stand during the late afternoon hours. If everything went as I suspected, my hunt would over long before legal shooting time expired. And I fully expected my archery tag would be adorning the antlers of a Pope & Young-class buck.

Shelves that run along the sides of hills can be great places for stand sites, but be fore-warned: Because of where they're found, shelves are also very susceptible to swirling wind conditions.

But as many bow-hunters know, when it comes to trophy-sized whitetails especially, even the best laid plans seldom work to perfection. Such was the case on this particular hunt. To make a long story much shorter, I didn't arrow a record book buck on opening day. I didn't even *see* a buck on that hunt. In fact, most of the archery season had passed into history before I saw one of the bucks again. The rut-possessed trophy was totally consumed with trailing a sweet-smelling doe. He passed by well out of bow range.

In my defense, the aforementioned incident took place a good number of years ago. However, it still serves as a painful but helpful reminder of the many intricacies involved in hunting for hill-country whitetails.

You see, the bachelor group of bucks I was watching resided in the wooded bluff country found near my home in west-central Wisconsin. Knowing very little about this particular aspect of hunting, I had simply walked in and set up my stand along the route I had witnessed the bucks using most often. It's now obvious that one or more of the bucks had figured out something was wrong the first time I hunted them.

What really bugged me at the time was that I had checked wind direction beforehand to make sure it would be to my advantage. It appeared to be perfect. So how were those bucks able to figure out I was there? Although it took a while, I eventually figured out that swirling winds were the culprit.

Hunting Hilltop Saddles

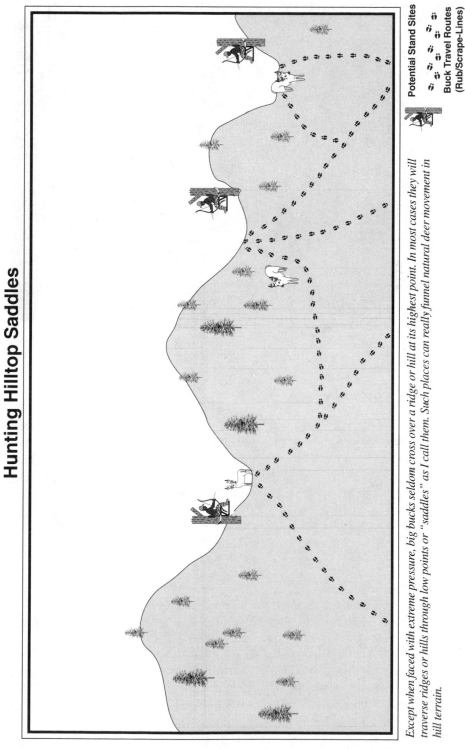

Potential Stand Sites

Buck Travel Routes
(Rub/Scrape-Lines)

Except when faced with extreme pressure, big bucks seldom cross over a ridge or hill at its highest point. In most cases they will traverse ridges or hills through low points or "saddles" as I call them. Such places can really funnel natural deer movement in hill terrain.

Whitetails access their ranges via the routes that offer the least resistance. This means that, when crossing over hills, deer are going to walk through the lowest points (saddles) on those hills.

Saddles and Flats

Interestingly, I now have two very productive stand sites in that same wooded bluff where I watched those six bucks many years ago. These stand sites were established only after I had spent many hours scouting and learning the intricacies of hill-country whitetail hunting. Once I understood the science of how the deer were relating to their environment, the pieces started falling into place.

One of my stands was located on the very top of the bluff, where a slight dip in the ridgeline created a natural saddle. The first year I hunted from the stand, I saw a bunch of different "non-shooter" bucks. But even without a kill to my credit, I still considered the season a rewarding one. I had learned that there was, indeed, a way to set up on hill-country whitetails without getting "picked-off" on every hunt.

As I've since learned, saddles can be real pockets of action in hilly terrain. The reason for this is quite simple. Remember, when accessing their ranges, undisturbed whitetails don't want to expend any more energy than necessary. When it comes time to decide where they should walk up and over hills, deer are going to choose the quickest and *easiest* routes. Saddles are the paths of least resistance for hill-country whitetails.

There are many instances in hill country when crop lands butt right up against the bottom of a steep, wooded hill. But I've also seen cases where an expanse of flat, wooded ground was situated between the bottom of the hill and the open ground. Some of these wooded flats were no more than 50 yards wide, but I've also seen and hunted some that were more than 200 yards in width.

Like mature bucks everywhere, hill-country trophies are notorious for departing open crop land some time before first light. But instead of heading straight back to their bedding areas, these deer often will hang-up in those wooded flats found between the fields and hills. They'll spend time on the flats rubbing, scraping or maybe even feeding on some in-woods food sources.

Because this activity can continue until well after daylight, morning hunts on these flats can be highly productive. The only criteria is that you set up in such a way that ensures you can slip into your stand sites undetected.

But this isn't to say that afternoon hunts in flats can't be equally as productive. In fact, I'm aware of a number of situations where big bucks showed up in flats some time before dark. These deer would then hang back in the timber, rubbing, scraping, sparring and browsing until darkness fell. Then they'd head out into the open crop land.

As those who hunt hill country can attest, flats also can be found along the tops of hills. Instead of merely breaking up and over, which is typical of a "hog's-back" contour feature, the hill flattens out on top. Just like the flats found along the bottoms, these hilltop flats can vary drasticially in size.

But regardless of their size or where they're found, flats usually play host to a great deal of buck activity. This activity can become quite intense during the final days of the pre-rut. However, it increases even more once the actual rut starts because antlerless deer spend a *lot* of time bedding, feeding and traveling on flats.

Still, there's yet another reason why even the biggest bucks feel relatively safe venturing onto flats. Because of the topographical and natural features present, mature deer know that if they're suddenly threatened on a flat, they can be out of harm's way in the blink of an eye.

On hilltop flats, a buck needs only to take a few bounds and he can be over the hill and out of sight from the threat. On flats found at the bottoms of hills, whitetails have a couple of options they can exploit when they feel threatened. They can either run out into the nearby open fields or they can simply melt into the thick brush that often borders the back edge of such flats.

The great thing about hunting on hilltop flats is that you can count on getting true winds. That's not always the case when hunting bottom flats, however. Just like when setting up on hillside shelves, you're going to need a wind that's blowing parallel to the hill bordering the back edge of the flat.

A couple of seasons back I shot a great buck during my home state's late archery season. On the day I shot the buck I was hunting in a flat area along the bottom of a rather small, but steep bluff. Now normally, the wind swirls terribly in this particular spot—except on those occasions when we get a brisk, northwest wind. And that's the exact sort of wind we had on that late December day two years ago. The heavy-beamed 8-pointer didn't have a clue I was anywhere in the area.

Gently sloping ridges or "fingers" are another place hill-country whitetails use with regularity.

Working the Fingers for Trophies

Another place to search for concentrated deer activity in hill country is on those gently sloping ridges (or "fingers" as I call them) that break away from a main hilltop and gradually descend to the valley below. These gently sloping fingers create a natural deer travel corridor, as they allow hill-country whitetails to, once again, travel about their ranges while expending the least amount of energy.

In my opinion, fingers rank right up there with saddles as the best places to ambush big bucks in hill-country. A word of caution: When setting up to hunt fingers, some thought must go into where your stands are placed.

To begin with, I would avoid setting up anywhere along the top of the finger, where the deer do the majority of their traveling. Even though these fingers might have a gradual slope, any buck walking down the finger still is going to be approaching from the "high side" of your stand site. In many cases this will put that deer nearly at eye level with you—regardless of how high you placed your tree stand!

I've found the best way to set up when hunting these fingers is to place your stand slightly off to one side of the top. You want to be just far enough from the top of the finger to avoid getting visually picked off. Yet you still want to be close enough so that you can make a sure, killing shot.

In recent years, we've found another tactic that can be extremely effective for taking hill-country whitetails during the rut. As most bow-hunters know, the most difficult aspect of hunting during this particular time frame is that bucks aren't in any real pattern. In fact, I've found the best definition of their behavior during the peak breeding period to be "helter-skelter."

Anyway, I had noticed for some time that rutting bucks spent a lot of time walking right along the edge of cropped fields, where they butt up against wooded hills/ bluffs. It finally dawned on me that what they're doing is cross-checking every runway that exits those fields. Just one quick sniff of each runway can tell them if an estrus doe has passed through that spot recently. If they find the scent they're looking for, they're immediately off on the trail of their future girlfriend.

Placing your stands along the bottom of a wooded hill, just in from the edge of the fields, can put you in position to cash in on some cross-trailing buck activity. And don't think for a second that the action is going to be exclusive to the early-morning/ late-afternoon hours. When big bucks are searching for receptive does, time of day means nothing. You're just as apt to see action at midday as at first or last light.

Finding Stand Sites in Hill Country

It's not difficult to locate potential hot spots in hill country. Yes, you can use topo maps to perhaps get you started in the right direction. But you can find the best places to search for potential stand sites merely by standing back some distance and looking at the lay of the land in your hunting area.

For instance, scanning the tops of distant ridgelines is a quick and easy way to locate saddles. You can also use this method to find those secondary ridges that break away from the main ridgeline and slope gently down to the valley below. Such places are bound to be the main travel routes for the local whitetail herd.

The great thing about this long-range, visual form of scouting is that it can be employed at any time of year. It makes no difference if foliage is present or not. You should be able to locate points of interest just as easily in September as in February.

It's a different story, however, when attempting to locate shelves or flats. Often, the change of elevation on features like shelves are so slight that they won't even show up on a topo map. And both flats and shelves often are impossible to find via the stand-back-and-look method. Hence, the only way to pinpoint the location of these places is by on-site investigation.

Whether morning stands should placed at the tops or bottoms of hills or somewhere in between is often dependent upon existing conditions. For example, in the hilly, agricultural country where I hunt, the majority of buck feeding occurs in fields located at the bottoms of the wooded hills. However, these bucks prefer to bed on or near the tops of the hills.

In the perfect scenario my morning stand will be situated along the route a mature buck is using to reach his bedding area after a night of feeding in the crop lands. However, this stand must be located far enough away from the crop land so I don't disturb that buck when walking into the spot. I stand my best chance of accomplishing this by establishing a stand site somewhere nearer the tops of the hills.

Should you place your stand at the very top or the very bottoms of hills? Or should it be placed somewhere in between? I'm afraid each individual hill-country situation calls for its own answer.

It's a bit different when searching out afternoon stands. For example, there might be times when you can get away with hunting on the edge of prime feeding areas. This is especially true if the deer you're hunting are relatively unpressured.

But if you go through a few evening stand sessions without seeing any activity by antlered animals, then it's time to relocate. My suggestion is to move uphill, which will put you just a little closer to bedding areas. As always when hunting hill-country, keep swirling winds in mind as you're looking for new stand sites.

The positioning of morning and evening stands also can be influenced by the presence of thermals. If you're hunting an area where thermals are present, then morning stands should be placed near the top of hills, evening stands at the bottom.

As you might have gathered, those who hunt whitetails in hill country are faced with just a bit more adversity than flatland deer hunters. But as I so painfully learned from that one hill-country hunt many years ago, there is a way of dealing with these adversities. All it takes is just a little more dedication and close adherence to a well-disciplined game plan.

Greg's Proven Pointers

- Take the time to study how hill-country deer access their ranges to provide you with the clues needed to hunt your areas most effectively.

- Hillside "shelves" will almost always be used as primary travel routes by deer.

- Deer perfer to cross up and over hills through those spots that afford them the least resistance. Therefore, low spots or "saddles" on hill/ridge tops act as natural funnels.

- The most important point to keep in mind about hunting hill-country whitetails is this: There are only so many places in this type of terrain where you can expect "true" winds.

CHAPTER SEVENTEEN

Whitetails— Weather or Not

When it comes to predicting deer movement, there's one topic that's bound to bring out more philosophies than any other—weather. I can guarantee that if you ask several deer hunters about how weather affects deer movement, you'll get several slightly different opinions.

What is the straight scoop on weather and whitetails? Is it true that deer *always* move around during periods of inclement weather? If so, then it's worthwhile to go out and sit on your stand even during torrential downpours. This also means you can expect to see deer running around kicking up their heels during severe winter blizzards. And it only stands to reason that deer are *really* going to move anytime the mercury plummets well below zero. Well, maybe and maybe not.

Much of the information I'm going to bring forth in this chapter regarding whitetails and weather has been gathered from 30-plus years of personal observations. However, this information should not be used as a strict guideline. Rather, hunters should consider the information to be reference material. For, as I've learned, whitetails don't *always* behave in the exact same manner, even under very similar weather conditions.

Rain

I've listed rain first because white-tailed deer hunters everywhere can expect to encounter rain. Because of this, there also are more theories on how rain affects deer movement than any other weather condition. From what I've seen, some of these theories are right on the money, but some aren't.

Whitetails often become very "feed active" during periods of light rain or drizzle. Interestingly, this activity could just as well occur at midday as midnight.

As far as I'm concerned, one of the best times to be out in the woods is during a light rain or drizzle. The main reason for this is that whitetails are prompted to get up and start feeding during periods of light rain or drizzle. Interestingly, these rain-activated feeding frenzies could just as well occur during midday as during early morning or late afternoon.

One positive aspect of hunting during light rain is that often you're able to keep your passage through the woods a secret. If you're a stand hunter, this means you should be able to reach your stand sites without alerting the deer to your presence. And if you're the type who prefers to still-hunt, this silent passage certainly will provide you with the opportunity to sneak up on more deer than usual.

Another positive thing I've noted about hunting during light rain is that the rain seems to wash away a good part of my human odor. I can't tell you the number of times I've had deer cut my tracks and/or walk around one of my stand sites during a light rain. Yet these deer never smelled me. I know it might have been a different story under dry conditions.

Hunting during rainy periods also has a negative side. With the woods saturated it's also possible the deer can sneak up on you. I can think of several big bucks that got by me because they never made a whisper of a sound. One in particular, a solid Pope & Young-class 10-pointer, actually walked within 10 yards of my stand site during a light rain. By the time I turned my head and saw him, he was 30 yards out and quickly walking away—no shot opportunity!

What about hunting during heavy downpours? I'm rather divided on my feelings. At times I think hunters would be much better off seeking shelter (as the deer often do) during periods of extremely heavy rain. But at other times, I think this might be the best time of all to try and shoot a big buck. Let me explain.

First of all, to take advantage of big buck opportunities, it's vitally important that our equipment be in *perfect* working order. Well, after more than just a couple of hunts in extremely heavy rain, I can tell you that it's just about impossible to keep your equipment in *perfect* working order.

For instance, I prefer to put feather-fletchings instead of plastic vanes on my hunting arrows. Even after they've been treated with the best waterproofing agents available, feathers remain waterproof only so long. And once they lose their ability to shed water, feathers quickly soak up moisture and become matted against the arrow shaft. Once this happens, your arrows will not fly true.

Those archers who use plastic vanes on their hunting arrows aren't immune from weather related problems, either. If everything on you and your bow—including cams, pulleys, wheels, cables, limbs, rest, etc.—is wet or water-coated, then your accuracy level probably will not be the same as under dry conditions.

And don't think for one second that hunting with a firearm will allow you to avoid such problems. If your firearm is equipped with a scope, I can almost guarantee the lenses will become water-streaked and/or fogged over (for some reason, this always seems to happen just before a big buck strolls into view).

Some readers would argue that using scope covers or constantly wiping off the lenses will keep you from running into these problems. Think again. If the rain is coming down hard enough—I'm talking about pouring down—then it's

My observations have shown me that whitetails—and all wildlife for that matter—simply "hole-up" during periods of heavy rainfall.

going to be nearly impossible, even with scope covers, to keep lenses clean and dry. And believe me, the big bucks I hunt aren't going to stand around and wait while I remove scope covers and wipe off the lenses.

The impact of hard rain can go beyond scopes on firearms. Several years ago I missed a good buck while hunting during a torrential downpour. Although my scope was a bit water streaked when the deer appeared, I could still see him well enough to get off an accurate shot—or so I thought. The reason I missed that deer was because some water had run down inside the barrel of my rifle. As I found out, this *can* affect bullet flight.

I think I've made it clear that I'm not a big fan of hunting during heavy rains. But there's another reason, aside from the obvious equipment problems: Deer don't move around a lot when rain is coming down in buckets.

If you've ever paid attention to wildlife activity, then you know most animals seek shelter during periods of heavy rain—they "hole-up," so to speak. And therein lies the reason I'm divided on whether or not I should be out and about while it's raining heavily.

If you know spots where deer hole-up during heavy rains, then you could be on your way to filling your tag. In my part of the country, deer often head for thick pine groves and other heavy-canopied forested areas when rainfall becomes intense. By setting up in or still-hunting through such spots while the rain is falling hardest, it's possible to end up within range of a big buck. (For some reason, whitetails don't seem to be quite as alert and attentive during periods of heavy rain.) But again, the obvious problem is keeping your equipment in good working order.

Snow

No other weather condition holds as much mystique for deer hunters as snow. Unfortunately, it also appears that no other weather condition is quite as misunderstood. After spending a good deal of my hunting career chasing whitetails in the snow, I think I've figured out why this is so.

For instance, I think most hunters are aware that deer movement picks up considerably during that 12 hour period immediately preceding a major snowfall. And whitetails often continue to move around while the snow is falling. But just like with rain, there are exceptions to this.

From what I've seen, whitetails often (but not *always*) seek shelter when a snowfall becomes extremely heavy. Thick pine forests, wind-sheltered hillsides and river/creek bottoms are just a few of the places where whitetails will seek respite from the harsh weather. Obviously, waiting in ambush or still-hunting through such places can be effective tactics when snow is falling heavily.

I've seen plenty of examples when a severe winter storm has lasted for a couple of days. In most cases, the deer I was hunting at the time quit moving while the storm was in progress. It was a different story, however, once the storm started moving out of the area.

After spending a day or two waiting out a storm, the first thing whitetails want to do is fill their bellies. And it doesn't matter if it's early morning, midday

Heavy snows can drastically alter the normal behavior and travel patterns of whitetails—even during the rut! My brother Jeff arrowed this big Manitoba buck after adjusting his hunting strategies accordingly.

or nighttime, once deer sense that a storm is starting to lessen in intensity, they're going to go grab some groceries.

And what kind of foods will they keying on? Whitetails that reside in farm country usually concentrate their feeding efforts on standing and/or freshly picked corn fields. Big woods deer, on the other hand, are going to seek out the nearest and freshest clear-cut areas. If the cut area is quite substantial in size, it's not unusual for a fairly large number of deer to spend the duration of the winter there.

The best times to be in the woods are during the 12-hour period just prior to when a major winter storm moves in, and then again during the 12-hour period just after the storm moves off. Even the biggest bucks in an area often can be seen moving about in broad daylight during these times, which means they are very killable.

Deer behavior and movement patterns can be somewhat predictable *once winter has actually set in.* However, it's a completely different story during those first snowfalls of the year. Unlike many hunters, I consider the presence of snow at this time of year more a liability than an asset.

I admit that snow cover increases one's visibility tremendously. And having snow on the ground can make reading and deciphering sign a snap. But personally—for my pre-rut and rut bow-hunts especially—I'd rather go without the "luxury" of a snow cover.

Why do I feel this way? Because the first significant snowfalls of the year change the habits and travel patterns of *all* deer in the affected area. Believe me, these changes don't necessarily work in a hunter's favor. My brother Jeff had an experience recently that illustrates this point.

Jeff was scheduled to spend the last couple of days of October and the first five days of November hunting in southern Manitoba. On the day Jeff arrived, it was raining. "But at some point during the night the rain turned to snow," he told me. "The snow continued to fall all the next day, and didn't quit until some time after dark that night. All in all, we ended up with right around six-inches on the ground." Perfect hunting conditions, right? Guess again!

The area where Jeff was hunting is made up of a rather large expanse of woods. This woods is bordered entirely on one side by crop land. Past hunts in this area had shown my brother and me that the deer bedded in the big woods, made their way to the crop lands in late afternoon, and then departed at first light in the morning. The pattern was a virtual no-brainer and easy to figure out.

"The snow cover changed all that, however," Jeff informed me. "Almost immediately the deer quit using the crop lands and instead got into a browse-oriented feeding pattern. Of course, this meant they weren't leaving the woods. But even worse than this was the fact that the snowfall drastically changed the way the deer *should* have been behaving at that time of year. The very obvious breeding behavior I was expecting to see never did materialize.

"I initially thought that the key was to find where some antlerless deer were feeding. I figured the big bucks would eventually show up in these same spots to check for hot does. But after hunting near concentrations of antlerless deer for several days and seeing only one small buck, it became obvious I had to change my tactics."

On the very last afternoon of his hunt, Jeff decided to try something different. "I relocated to a spot that was way back off the beaten path, in some real heavy cover. A half-hour after getting settled in my portable tree stand, a big buck walked into sight. The buck was merely browsing, not displaying any kind of rut behavior whatsoever. Eventually, he ended up walking by just 15 yards from where I was sitting."

The big 6x4 typical Jeff arrowed had a gross score near 150-points. We estimated the buck to be 3-1/2 years-old, which meant he should have been a prolific breeder. But interestingly, instead of being stained a deep brown, the buck's hock glands were still snow-white in color, a sure indication that the deer hadn't been spending much time making or freshening scrapes. "It's obvious the six-inches of fresh snow had, at least for the time being, put the rut on hold," Jeff stated.

My brother's experience isn't an isolated case either. I can't tell you the number of times when a snowfall has ruined what had otherwise been some quality pre-rut and rut hunting conditions. I've taken great pains to figure out exactly what the deer I'm hunting will be eating at different times during the season. Because normally we don't receive significant snowfalls in late October and early November, I assume the deer will be relating to "bare-ground" food sources.

It's usually not a big deal trying to figure out where farm country deer relocate their feeding efforts after we get a bit of snow. It's a different story, however, when dealing with big woods whitetails. The sudden appearance of several inches of early fall snow can prompt these animals to pack up and move some distance— maybe even several miles! Unless you're extremely familiar with the area, or have

There's a lot more to whitetails and the weather than can be covered in one chapter. Suffice to say that changes in the weather affect the way deer behave.

dealt with similar situations in the past, you could spend valuable time during the best part of the season just trying to find where the deer have gone.

Another thing about those first snowfalls of the year. I stated earlier that our visibility increases substantially when there's a snow cover. But remember, the deer also are afforded this same luxury. They can now see you and watch your every move from even greater distances than before.

Lastly, some hunters are under the impression that the first snow cover of the year stimulates deer to do more moving around during daylight hours. "They like to run around and kick up their heels," a hunter told me recently. Wrong! If anything, the fact that everything around them is suddenly white seems to make deer a bit paranoid. It's almost as if they realize that their natural camouflage isn't quite as effective, and that *any* predator can now spot them rather easily.

Whitetails will eventually grow accustomed to having snow cover and adjust their patterns and behavior accordingly. Unfortunately, this three- or four-day adjustment period often occurs during the best part of the hunting season, i.e., the rut. This means it's entirely possible you could miss out on some great action. Like I said, having a snow cover isn't *always* a blessing!

Extremely Cold Weather

As with hunting whitetails in snow, I've found that cold weather deer hunting also generates a lot of interest. Surprisingly, a great deal of this interest seems to come from Southern deer hunters who find it interesting that some of us "Yankees" actually hunt during bouts of extremely cold weather. But, to be honest, I've found this a *very* productive time to be in the woods.

I think it's important to explain what I mean by "extremely cold weather." In northern latitudes, extremely cold weather is anything 0°F or colder. However, this same rule of thumb doesn't apply in Southern latitudes. What should Southern hunters consider "extremely cold weather?" The best answer I can give is temperatures far below what is considered normal for the time of year in question.

In the Northern areas where I hunt, there is a lot of deer feeding activity when temperatures are in the 0°F to -30°F range. It makes no difference whether these kinds of temperatures happen upon us during the rut (which they often do) or during our late archery season. When the mercury hits zero or below, I'm going to be out in the woods.

I concentrate the majority of my cold-weather hunting along the routes that deer use to travel back and forth between bedding and feeding areas. I use this same approach regardless of whether I'm dealing with a pre-rut, rut, or post-rut situation. Whitetails place a *lot* of importance on eating when it gets *really* cold.

Most hunters will agree with me that cold weather definitely prompts whitetails to move. But I've also had some hunters tell me that the colder it gets, the better. As far as they're concerned, it can't get too cold. Well, take it from some one who knows—yes it can! In fact, there are times when it gets so cold that hunting is not only a very unsafe endeavor, it's also quite impractical.

Once temperatures start edging lower than -30°F, and if these temperatures stay for some length of time, deer movement will decrease noticeably. In fact, we've even seen instances where, because they didn't want to expend any more energy than absolute necessary, big bucks would bed down right on the edge of primary feeding areas during long bouts of brutally cold weather. These deer would continue to bed right next to their food sources until the cold snap came to an end.

This is exactly what I meant about extremely cold weather causing impractical hunting situations. Anytime whitetails bed very close to where they're eating it's darn near impossible to set-up on those animals. I've seen situations where deer would lay on hillsides slightly above the feeding area. From that position they were able to keep watch over everything that was going on around them.

And lest you think these deer occasionally wander off some distance to feed in other areas, forget it. We usually have a fairly heavy snow cover during our coldest weather. By continually checking tracks and runways, we've been able to ascertain that, in many cases, the deer were spending *all* their time within a couple of hundred yards of a specific food source.

Whitetails seem to know that the extremely cold temperatures already are sapping their precious energy. Any unnecessary or extensive movement will only drain these energy reserves even more, and they can sorely afford to lose *any* energy at such a stressful time. Consequently, the deer drastically reduce their movements, while at the same time trying to take in adequate amounts of highly nutritious foods.

There is more to whitetails and the weather than the things I've brought forth in this chapter—I could have written a rather lengthy chapter purely on hunting

Whitetails place a lot of importance on eating when the temperature drops. But it's important to note that brutally cold temperatures can make for extremly tough hunting conditions. Take it from someone who knows, there is such a thing as too cold.

deer in snow. I also could have written much more about hunting in rain and during cold weather, but that wasn't my intent.

Rather, I wanted to address what I thought were some of the more important points about hunting whitetails in rain, snow and cold weather. Hopefully, I've covered some things that you'll find beneficial on future hunts.

It has long been my belief that deer hunters can solve many of the problems confronting them merely by applying a bit of common sense. This is never more true than when trying to figure out what sort of an approach to employ when facing changing weather conditions. Stop, give it a bit of thought and then act accordingly.

Greg's Proven Pointers

- There are a lot of theories about how different weather conditions affect deer behavior and movement. Some of these theories are right on the money, some aren't.

- Rainy weather can prompt whitetails into feed-active movement patterns. But this activity will cease abruptly if rainfall becomes too heavy.

- Just like rain, a little snow can be a good thing. However, a bunch of snow can be detrimental to our chances for success—especially if these heavy snows occur during the rut!

- Yes, deer activity often does increase during periods of cold weather. But believe me, it can get too cold! My observations have shown that deer often "hunker down" and refuse to move when temperatures become brutally cold.

CHAPTER EIGHTEEN

More Than A Feeling

I've never really felt that I possessed any sort of sixth sense. Nor do I consider myself some sort of a psychic. But I can state without hesitation that there are times when I'm deer hunting that I get the "feeling" something is going to happen. What's most interesting, and sometimes even a bit scary, is that I usually get these feelings some time before I first hear or see a deer.

I've been aware for quite some time that this sort of thing happens to me. But for fear that I might be labeled some sort of a wacko (which may be the case yet), I never mentioned my "feelings" to anyone. However, time has changed all that.

What made me change my mind and come clean about my "feelings?" It's because I've spent so much time over the past 10 years talking to other deer hunters. I've found that deer hunters, for the most part, are a pretty honest and straightforward bunch. They'll tell you just about anything you want to know, with the possible exception of *exactly* where their stand sites are located.

Because of this overall honest demeanor, it has been no problem for me to determine that there are one heck of a lot of deer hunters who, like me, get the "feeling." As you might imagine, this information played a huge role in my finally coming clean about some of my past experiences with the phenomenon.

There are people who are going to read this chapter and nod their heads in total agreement. Those people have no doubt had their own personal experiences with the "feeling." But I'm fully aware that there probably are far more people who are going to read this chapter and come away shaking their heads in disbelief. Perhaps these individuals think I'm some kind of nut who belongs in a padded room, attired in one of those nice white jackets with the sleeves that buckle behind the back.

My brother Mike poses proudly with a big buck his son, Isaac, shot a few years ago. Did Isaac end up in the right spot because of a "feeling?"

Such reaction is totally understandable. I know from plenty of past confrontations that there are a lot of people who have never experienced the "feeling." And they never will—too bad.

Those people who do experience the "feeling" are more in tune with everything that's going on around them while they're hunting. Does this make them better hunters? Well, let me put it this way: Almost all of the highly successful hunters I know admit they are aware of some sort of extra sense. Interestingly, they also state that this sense surfaces only when they're hunting.

On the other hand, I know plenty of other deer hunters who are only moderately or even less successful. Almost every one of these individuals gives me a funny look when I ask them about the "feeling." Such a reaction leaves no doubt in mind that they've never experienced it.

You Don't Always Feel It, But When You Do...

I must admit that I don't get the "feeling" every time I head into the woods. There are far more times when I feel nothing at all. But at other times, the "feeling" is so strong that it's almost frightening.

For instance, there was that time back in 1974. It was opening day of my home state's gun season for deer. I was sitting on a stand that had been placed on a wooded hillside, perhaps 100 yards from the edge of a second year re-growth area.

For some odd reason, I kept turning my head and looking between two huge poplar trees at this one small opening. Previous scouting had shown me there were no runways or buck sign anywhere near the opening. And it hurt my neck to turn my head enough to see the opening. So why did I keep looking that way?

That question was answered the next time I twisted my head and looked into the opening. A big whitetail buck was standing there looking back at me. Not daring to make a move, I played a game of stare-down with the deer. The game lasted less than 15 seconds, then the buck decided he'd seen enough. He made a successful escape by keeping just enough trees between him and me.

I stayed on my stand a couple of hours more on that opening morning back in 1974. During those two hours I thought a lot about why I had kept looking (staring actually) at the spot where the buck eventually showed up. It was as if I knew he was going to appear right there. I had gotten a certain "feeling" about it.

The next time I remember getting the "feeling" was three years later. Again, it was opening morning of the firearm season for deer. Ironically, I was set up in the same area where I'd had the stare-down with the buck three years earlier. This time, however, I was determined to make sure that I would see any buck coming into the area *before* he saw me.

The day dawned clear and very cold. There was no snow on the ground, which made the leaves laying on the ground as crunchy as a fresh batch of potato chips. I knew it would be virtually impossible for any deer to sneak up on me today.

I had been on my stand for about 30 minutes when, exactly as I had figured, I heard a deer coming my way. It took a good three or four minutes, however, before I saw it. A quick check through my scope confirmed that it was a doe.

The antlerless animal slowly picked her way on by me, stopping occasionally to scan the area and sniff the air for danger. Having had some practice in the routine, I alertly watched behind her for any sign of a buck. But 20 minutes after the doe had disappeared, I decided that there wasn't a buck following on her trail. Leaning my gun against a nearby tree, I reached into my pocket for a candy bar. I unwrapped it as quietly as possible.

The candy bar was only about half finished when, suddenly, I got the "feeling." I hadn't heard anything, I hadn't seen anything, but the "feeling" was so strong that I dropped the rest of my candy bar on the ground and grabbed my rifle. My heart was pounding and my eyes were riveted to a spot about 70 yards away. For some unknown reason, I just knew that something was about to happen.

Before long I heard the unmistakable sounds of a deer walking in the frozen leaves. The sounds were coming from an area just beyond where I was already looking. And then, as if my magic, a beautiful 8-point buck walked into my sight—exactly where I had been staring for the past few minutes!

The big deer's neck was swollen to the point where it looked almost ridiculous. His tall, evenly matched set of antlers fairly glistened in the early morning sunlight. The buck made quite a sight as he walked slowly along, obviously absorbed by the feelings of peak rut. It was no problem anchoring him with one well-placed shot.

It was while I was standing over my prize and admiring his rack that I began to think about that "feeling" I had before I had first heard the buck approaching. It was the same sort of "feeling" I had on opening morning in 1974 before the buck I'd seen that day had appeared. Admittedly, the whole deal was a bit scary. But I merely shook my head and began the chore of field-dressing the 8-pointer. Any further though of my possessing some sort of sixth sense disappeared when I started dragging my buck out of the woods. My only thought was wishing for somebody to help me.

Later that same morning, as I was turning onto the driveway of my hunting cabin, I started thinking about the "feeling." I wondered if I dared tell any of the other members of my hunting party about it. I decided against it.

After all, it wasn't an easy a thing to describe or explain. I didn't know for sure how I felt when the "feeling" was upon me, so how could I ever explain it to someone else? I dismissed the idea, vowing never to tell anyone about the "feeling." For all I knew, it was probably nothing anyway. But then three years later, during our archery season for deer, it happened again.

Premonitions of Approaching Trophies

It was an early November afternoon. The sun had slipped beneath the treeline and that distinct evening chill was slowly easing into the air. I was beginning to feel the pains so familiar to anyone who has spent an extended amount of time on a tree stand. In fact, I was in the process of trying to work a cramp out of my right leg when the "feeling" came over me.

My attention was immediately drawn to an area about 60 yards away. Before long, I made out the form of a deer walking in my direction. I soon distinguished it as a doe, and behind her was a fawn. The fawn was displaying a very nervous demeanor and kept looking back over its rump. Shortly, I saw the reason why. A huge-bodied buck walked into view, trailing behind the two antlerless deer.

The doe and fawn continued on a course that eventually brought them within 20 yards of my stand site. But the buck would come no closer on this day. He stopped just outside of my effective range and went to work demolishing a small tree with his antlers. He was still rubbing on that tree when legal shooting time expired.

On the drive back to my cabin I started thinking about the "feeling" I had experienced again. I had no doubt that there was something to it. I somehow knew the big buck was going to appear almost five minutes before he actually did. What's more, I seemed to have a good premonition of *where* he was going to come into sight. The hair on the back of my neck was standing up. Was this weird or what? But as I was about to find out the next day, I hadn't seen anything yet.

I arrived at my stand site 15 minutes before daylight. A half-hour later, a small buck passed by my stand. Other than that, the only thing stirring around me were dozens of squirrels who were busy finding and burying as many acorns as they could before the first snowfall buried their precious food supply.

After being on my stand for nearly three hours, I had just about decided that the big buck was going to show. But then it happened yet again. The "feeling"

Not all my "feelings" have resulted in me affixing my tag to a big buck. But just enough of them have to make it worth talking about.

was back, and this time it wasn't fooling around. It was so overpowering that I began to get worried. At one point, I even contemplated climbing down from my stand and heading out of the woods. Fortunately for me, I decided against doing that. Instead, I grabbed my bow and got ready for whatever happened next. I didn't have long to wait.

I first heard him coming when he was still a good 200 yards away. It was the sounds of a deer trotting through the crunchy, frozen oak leaves. For some unexplainable reason, I knew the deer's destination was the very tree where I sat waiting.

The sight of the big-bodied buck coming up and over a small rise 50 yards away is something I'll never forget. The morning sun was gleaming off his polished antlers, and I could see his powerful muscles rippling under his slick hide. Every time the buck exhaled, twin columns of steam could be seen escaping from his nostrils. It seemed he was grunting with each step he took.

When the buck got to a range of 15 yards I drew my bow. He took two more steps and the arrow was on its way. The buck spun around immediately as the arrow found its mark. I watched him run away through the relatively open oak forest. There was no doubt I was looking at a fatally hit animal.

The buck's rack sported 8 points and had an inside spread of more than 17 inches. But as I had first noticed, it was his body size that was so impressive. After field-dressing, the buck weighed in at 215 pounds. His neck measured almost 32 inches around the middle and 30 inches right behind the ears.

A lot of time and effort went into my getting that deer, and he's a trophy that I'll remember for a long, long time. I'll also remember for a long time the "feeling" I got that morning, just before the monster deer trotted into view.

You Never Know When It's Going to Hit You

Some hunters I've talked with have admitted that they've gotten the "feeling" well ahead of time. Others have told me they knew something was going to happen when they first awoke on the day they killed a buck. It was almost as if a voice inside them was saying "Today is the day!"

Still other hunters have told me they were driving down the road when, all of a sudden, a sense of urgency to be on their stand came over them. My brother, Jeff, had just such an experience some years ago during our archery season.

Jeff was about halfway to his hunting area when he got the "feeling." He pushed the accelerator just a bit closer to the floor and sped to his destination. My brother hurriedly organized his gear, locked and closed the door of his vehicle and began to walk to his stand site. But after going only about 100 yards—and for some reason still unknown to him—Jeff broke into a trot. He ran the remaining distance to his stand and, without hesitation, scurried up the oak tree to where his stand had been placed.

Less than a minute later, he heard deer approaching his position. As they strolled into view, he could see that it was two does. Jeff could also see, by the way the does were acting, that another deer was following. After about a 15-second wait, Jeff could hear the unmistakable sounds of a rutting buck. Deep-pitched, pig-

My son Jacob is shown with a big buck I arrowed during a recent season. Even though my buddies urged me to give up on this stand site, I stuck with it. Something about the spot just "felt" right.

like grunts reverberated through the woodlot as the 8-pointer, hair standing on end, tracked the does toward my brother's ambush point. At 30 yards, the buck stopped broadside, giving Jeff the chance he wanted. Unfortunately, his arrow went wide of its intended target and all three deer raced out of sight.

Jeff had been in his stand less than five minutes. If it hadn't been for the fact that he had gotten that "feeling" while driving down the road, he probably wouldn't have seen those deer. I had a similar experience during a recent season here in Wisconsin.

I had been hunting a good-sized buck quite hard for much of the season. I knew the location of several of the buck's rub-lines and also where he was bedding. Still, try as I might, I couldn't get so much as a glimpse of the deer. His huge tracks and fresh rubs continued to taunt me.

Finally, I decided to give myself a break from the deer and try hunting a different area. I didn't get halfway to the new area I was planning to hunt, however, when, for some unexplainable reason, I slammed on the brakes of my pickup, turned around and raced back to the place where I had been hunting. To make a long story short, I shot the long sought-after buck 20 minutes after getting settled in my tree stand. The "feeling" had been there again.

Make Sure You Follow That Feeling

My biggest bow-killed buck to date, an 18-point non-typical monster, came about as the result of a "feeling." In the case of that deer, however, I didn't get the "feeling" mere minutes before he showed up. Rather, it came hours prior to my hunt, while I was sitting in my office pounding out the manuscript for a magazine article.

I managed to work in my office until around 1:30 p.m. Then I shut down my computer, hurriedly took a shower, got dressed and grabbed my hunting gear. The "feeling" was there all the while I was preparing for my hunt. Something good was going to happen on this day.

I was in my truck and just starting to back out of the garage when a pick-up pulled into my driveway. The truck belonged to my brother Mike. I knew Mike had just returned from a very successful mountain lion hunt in Montana. I also knew he had shot some quality video footage on that hunt. No doubt he had stopped by to show me the footage.

Now, there probably were a lot of times when it would have been *real* easy for me to sacrifice my day's hunt. But not so on this day. Man, the "feeling" had been there, nagging at the back of my mind, just about the entire day. I quickly explained to Mike that I just *had* to get out on my stand. Two hours later the non-typical was standing a mere 15 yards from my treestand. As they say, the rest is history.

What's most interesting about this whole thing is the way Mike reacted to my behavior. Normally, my brother would have tried to convince me that it wouldn't take long to look at the footage, or that there were plenty of days left in the season. Not so on this day; I believe Mike could sense the urgency I was feeling.

I think it's important to mention that my "feelings" don't seem to be restricted only to bucks. There have been many occasions when my sixth sense has warned

The smile on my brother's face says it all: Jeff is truly appreciative and respectful of the majestic animal lying before him. Remember, it's crucial to the future of this sport that our hunting endeavors remain healthy and fun.

me that a deer was going to appear, only to have an antlerless animal (or several) walk into view. If there was a buck somewhere around, I didn't see him.

I should mention also that the special "feelings" I get aren't reserved only for those times when a deer is about to show up either. There have been occasions when I've experienced the same sort of sensation when scouting an area. For instance, I can't tell you the number of times when a distinct "feeling" forced me to check out part of a woods I would have otherwise overlooked. More times than not, those spots harbored more big buck sign than any of the surrounding cover.

There also have been times when the "feeling" has surfaced when I was searching for a stand site. This has happened dozens of times. I've been prompted to put my portable stand in a tree simply because it felt right. There was no great abundance of buck sign or anything else that would indicate the deer were walking through this spot. Yet, there was something about the place that seem to cry out, "This is it!" Over time I've learned that it's wise to trust these "feelings."

I remember one such stand-site I discovered through a "feeling." Over a 10-year period, two of my brothers and I managed to harvest a half-dozen bucks from that one spot—it was a real honey-hole!

During our archery season one year I shot a nice buck while sitting on the stand. A friend of mine volunteered to help me get the buck out of the woods. When I showed him where my stand was located he looked around a bit and then asked, "What the heck ever possessed you to put your stand here of all places." All I could do was shrug my shoulders, look him in the eye and reply, "It just felt right." I'm afraid my friend didn't understand. Of course, this guy will readily admit he's never had the "feeling" either.

I certainly don't have what I would consider a credible explanation for what causes the "feeling." I only know, after talking to a lot of deer hunters, that it *is* a very real thing. I'm also at a loss to explain why some people have it and some don't. And that's the way it seems to go with this thing: Either you have it or you don't. You can't fake it, nor can you practice at it to try and make it appear at your beck and call.

For those people who do, indeed, get the "feeling,", it can be used as a very effective method of controlling a bout of buck fever. If I'm warned five minutes in advance that a deer is going to show up, I use that five minutes to try and calm myself enough so that I will be totally prepared to take my shot, if and when the opportunity presents itself.

Of course, there are those hunters who are only going to get a worse case of buck fever if they have more than the normal amount of warning that a deer is headed their way. I'm afraid that nothing, not even ESP, will help those poor souls.

If you've read this entire book, then you'll have to agree that this chapter is very unlike any other. After the many pages of "how-to" stuff found in preceding chapters, I wanted to leave readers with something that would stimulate their thought process in a slightly different way. But more than anything, it was my intent to prove there still are some things about this sport that we don't know. I sincerely hope it stays that way.

In closing I would like to state that there's something very important *all* deer hunters need to keep in mind. It's okay if a healthy, personal competition exists between you and your quarry. However, you should never let a fierce and unhealthy competition between you and other hunters be the driving force behind your motivation for pursuing big deer.

Killing whitetail bucks should *never* turn into something we do simply because we're looking to win contests or gain status amongst our peers. Remember, when hunting ceases being fun and instead turns into something we feel we must do to impress others, then it's time to reevaluate our priorities.

I have a "feeling" most of you will agree!

If you enjoyed *Proven Whitetail Tactics*, then you'll definitely want to read Greg Miller's first book, *Aggressive Whitetail Hunting*. Here's what satisfied hunters have to say:

"I read your book, *Aggressive Whitetail Hunting*, and thought it was great! I now understand rubs and scrapes for what they really are."
> Joseph Cafiso
> Philadelphia, Pennsylvania

"You've nailed it! I personally think *Aggressive Whitetail Hunting* is the "Holy Bible" of whitetail hunting. Congratulations and thanks!"
> Al Drangstveit
> Taylor, Wisconsin

"After reading *Aggressive Whitetail Hunting* I shot a 212-pound, 11-point buck on the first day of our gun season. Your book definitely has given me a better understanding of big buck behavior."
> Greg Kinser
> Bowling Green, Kentucky

"I just finished reading your book, *Aggressive Whitetail Hunting*. Great job!! I like what you said and the way you said it. Well done and well written."
> Larry Weishuhn
> Uvalde, Texas

"Enclosed you'll find a photo of my first bow-killed buck, a fine 9-pointer. Reading your book, *Aggressive Whitetail Hunting*, gave me many valuable tips which contributed to my successful season. Thanks Greg!"
> Mike Tucker
> Cottage Grove, Minnesota

"I have read your book, *Aggressive Whitetail Hunting*, several times. Greg, you truly are one of the best writers in the country on the subject of whitetails, and one of my favorite authors."
> Joe Bucher
> Eagle River, Wisconsin

"I was most pleased with your book, *Aggressive Whitetail Hunting*, as it gave me something I have long been looking for. A discussion of hunting big woods whitetails from someone who truly is knowledgeable on the subject. Thanks very much!"
> Stuart Genung
> Monroe, Connecticut

Call Krause Publications today and order your copy of *Aggressive Whitetail Hunting*.

SHARE THE HUNTING SECRETS OF THE PROFESSIONALS!

Aggressive Whitetail Hunting
with Greg Miller teaches you how to hunt trophy bucks in public forests and farmlands, as well as in exclusive hunting lands. It's the perfect approach for gun and bow hunters who don't have the time or finances to hunt exotic locales. 6x9 SC • 208p • 80 photos
• **AWH01 $14.95**

Whitetail: Behavior Through the Seasons
offers in-depth coverage of whitetail behavior through striking portraits by award-winning photographer and author Charles J. Alsheimer. His in-the-field observations will help you better understand this spectacular game animal. 9x11-½ HC • 208p • 166 color photos • **WHIT $34.95**

Whitetail: The Ultimate Challenge
unlocks deer hunting's most intriguing secrets. Find insights on where and how to hunt whitetails across North America. Plus, Charlie Alsheimer helps you become a better outdoor photographer, too. 6x9 SC • 223p • 150 photos
• **WUC01 $14.95**

Hunting Mature Bucks
unleashes one of North America's top white-tailed deer authorities on those big, elusive bucks. Learn about hunting and herd management techniques from Larry Weishuhn. 6x9 SC • 213p • 80 photos • **HMB01 $14.95**

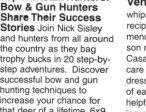

Secret Strategies From North America's Top Whitetail Hunters: Bow & Gun Hunters Share Their Success Stories
Join Nick Sisley and hunters from all around the country as they bag trophy bucks in 20 step-by-step adventures. Discover successful bow and gun hunting techniques to increase your chance for that deer of a lifetime. 6x9 SC • 240p • 80+ photos
• **GBT01 $14.95**

The Complete Venison Cookbook
whips up delicious new recipes and complete menus for your next venison meal. Jim and Ann Casada cover the proper care of meat and field dressing, health benefits of eating venison and helpful hints for easy, inexpensive dining. 6x9 Comb-bound • 208p
• **CVC $12.95**

Credit Card Calls Toll-free
800-258-0929 Dept. OAB1
Monday-Friday, 7 a.m. - 8 p.m. • Saturday, 8 a.m. - 2 p.m., CST
Visit our web site: http://www.krause.com/outdoors

Recomended by the editors at
DEER & DEER HUNTING MAGAZINE

SATISFACTION GUARANTEE
If for any reason you are not completely satisfied with your purchase, simply return it within 14 days and receive a full refund, less shipping.